FICTION NON FICTION

Volume 1

co-edited by
Bruno Zhu & Chisenhale Gallery

Contents

Editor's note

This reader brings together a collection of reprinted essays. Passages have been translated into English, included for reference within corresponding footnotes. Every effort has been made to preserve the integrity of the original works, and while some edits have been made for consistency across the texts, no further modifications have been made to the original meaning or intent of the authors' essays.

Foreword

Theoretical practice, practical theory

Zoé Whitley

At Chisenhale Gallery, we pride ourselves on 'critical proximity', which we position as the antithesis of critical distance. Working over an eighteen to twenty-four-month period, our process of realising an artist's new commission is as vital as the resulting ideation, and produces truly fascinating insights. Not only do we learn something about who an artist is – what they like to eat, which bag they prefer to carry when travelling (red Undercover x Eastpak jacket-backpack hybrid in Bruno Zhu's case), songs they enjoy listening to during install – but also we learn about what has shaped who the artist has become; from the inspirations germinated by fellow artists to the texts that inform their thinking, making, and being. The internet unreliably informs me that Albert Einstein had a famous quote: 'In theory, theory and practice are the same. In practice, they are not'.[1] More plausibly re-attributed to Benjamin Brewster, I nonetheless find this adage to be perpetually true in the course of our exhibition making. Many notions that underpin the work might be unseen but felt. Literary references would go unread unless brought to light in citation. For this reason, Volume I of Zhu's new reader *Fiction Non Fiction* is a particular gift, as we can all gain a nearness to the artist through the selected writings that have left their mark on his intellectual formation. Thank you Bruno, for personalising your artistic journey through this theoretical engagement.

Zhu's art starts with mood and objects to build new worlds. I was struck by the way art critic Matthew Bowman writes of *De-Distancing* art-historical time, noting that a substantial lag between past and present is usually 'the precondition for, and the mechanism by which to carry out a scholarly and properly critical art history; it also serves as a "mood" which stakes our attachment to objects and world'.[2] Zhu requires no such conventional arm's length – and indeed did not wait for permission – to engage in scholarly and curatorial activities, using A Maior, his family's clothing and home furnishings store in Viseu, Portugal. As an incubator for curatorial projects and critical enquiry, A Maior became a host for activations that ranged from exhibitions that following the cycle of ready-to-wear seasons to a programme that hosted an in-store opera singer-in-residence. Those actions ascribe a heightened sense of emotion and observation to our critical faculties and extend into Zhu's transformation of Chisenhale Gallery into an enfilade of immersive environments. Let us consider this volume as another realm, beyond the exhibition space, where we as readers can see and understand differently.

This volume assembles many great minds and writings. It was assembled by other great minds who comprise our brilliant team. Chisenhale Gallery Commissions Curator, Olivia Aherne and Asymmetry Curatorial Research Fellow, Rachel Be-Yun Wang have steered this ambitious publication with the essential support of Assistant Curator, Oscar Abdulla and Managing Editor, Anita Dawood. As ever, we are grateful to Sir Frank Bowling and Lady Rachel Scott for their generosity toward Chisenhale Gallery publishing. We steadily benefit from the mind-meld resulting from working with Mousse as co-publishers. Special thanks to designer Enver Hadzijaj and we look forward to Volume II with CAM - Centro de Arte Moderna Gulbenkian.

1 https://quoteinvestigator.com/2018/04/14/theory/ Accessed: 1 October 2024.

2 Matthew Bowman. 'Shapes of Time: Melancholia, Anachronism, De-Distancing' in Amanda Boetzkes and Aron Vinegar (eds.), *Heidegger and the Work of Art History*, (Farnham and Burlington: Ashgate, 2014), pp. 177.

Introduction

Bruno Zhu

A few years ago, after getting onto a busy tram in Amsterdam, I was greeted by the conductor.

'Konnichiwa!' he said. People around him laughed.

I happen to have experienced this many times before, as have many other Asian presenting people out there, I suspect. These Far East verbal nuggets – 'konnichiwa', 'pikachu', 'ni hao', 'xie xie' – are thrown at us in acts of recognition. They are delivered with an unnerving smile, one that hides their discomfort towards our very presence. By speaking 'my' language, the speaker simulates a form of inclusion: one premised by the rosy contract of a tolerant multiculturalism. And isn't tolerance a categorically positive trait in modern liberal culture? That same tolerance that inspires a conveyance of ironic niceties, backhanded compliments, and terms of endearment to dispel what may look 'awkward'; what may look 'strange'. Whatever I pose to them – a curiosity, threat, or both – becomes null when my alleged foreignness is voiced in their terms. It becomes about control.

It doesn't matter which Asian country these speakers refer to because further specificity begs for knowledge they don't possess. They don't know which Asian country they want to place me in, nor the language spoken there. Calling attention to that would make them lose face, reveal that they are not in control of 'my story', and in turn, that they are not in control of their own.

I bit my tongue and looked away after the conductor greeted me. I was ready to ignore him, but something was different this time. I noticed he wasn't the usual white European, he was Black. Yet he was still performing their racism – a ventriloquist act. According to mainstream anti-racist creed, a person of colour is a supposed ally. Yet, I felt betrayed. He was sitting in his booth surrounded by a cluster of passengers visibly entertained by his antics. Their laughter stung hard, so much so that it jolted me to turn to him and ask:

'What did you say?' The laughter in the carriage faded as I walked towards him asking my question again.

He giggled and said he was saying hello in 'my' language.

'But I'm not Japanese', I said.

To everyone's delight, he went on to name countries in East Asia followed by random words he knew in their respective languages.

'But I'm not from Asia', I interrupted, and the carriage fell back into silence.

'Then where are you from?' he asked, still with a grin on his face.

A white man on my left intervened, trying to excuse the conductor's act as innocent play. I told him to stay out of it.

People around us became increasingly uncomfortable. A young white couple that had been laughing were now holding each other dearly, dreading an imminent fight.

I often recall this interaction when I think about racial frameworks and how their dynamics play out today. I single out the players – the Black Dutch conductor, a group of white or white-passing passengers, and myself – and the central question that hung in the air: *if I'm not Asian, then what am I?*

I'm interested in the racist dispositions implied in their actions. In exchange for boarding the carriage, I was given an orientalist utterance as my welcome. By refusing it, I also refused the carriage's racialising assumptions, designating me an unpredictable subject. 'Such is the stuff that racecraft is made of. It occupies a middle ground between science and superstition, an invisible realm of collective understandings, a half-lit zone of the mind's eye'[1] write historian Barbara and sociologist Karen Fields on the conjuring of race. It is the practice of racism that produces race, and not the other way around. The Field sisters assert that racism is rooted in *ascribed* ancestry, an empty value form created by societal perception and cultural claims rather than self-identification. They describe the writings of Founding Father Thomas Jefferson, who painstakingly charted the 'race' of enslaved Africans:

> 'His catalogue of differences went from skin colour (they do not blush) and internal organs ("They secrete less by the kidnies [sic]"), to intellect ("In imagination, they are dull, tasteless, and anomalous") and even emotion" ("Their griefs are transient," he asserted without irony). Even so, as a man of science, Jefferson qualified: "I advance it therefore as a suspicion only that the blacks, whether originally a distinct race, or made distinct by time and circumstances, are inferior to the whites in the endowments both of body and mind."'[2]

Therefore what is interpreted as a priori – one's 'race' – is the outcome of a repeated practice of racism. Racism was and is applied to the implementation of inhuman modes of labour division, the killing of Indigenous peoples, the brutal extraction of resources, land theft, and the suppression of inter-class solidarity by colonial empires.

Yet the workings of 'racecraft' have programmed 'race', the act of the perpetrator, into a characteristic of the target.[3] The submission of the individual to racial capitalism becomes total when people start believing in, and taking ownership of, projected racial identities.

Volume I of this reader sits precisely at this juncture, between the unfolding of colonial histories and stories of racialisation. It proposes a close reading of works of fiction and non-fiction to understand how identity politics have been narrativised by liberal institutions. That very form of narrative can both continue or undo racial constructs and dynamics. The texts in this volume observe racially coded spaces and their proficiency in arranging bodies, ideas, and citizens according to the interests of the empire.

From Martinique to colonial Algeria, from Jamaican plantations to 1970s Lisbon, from a Shakespearian play to a late-18th century Atlantic autobiography, the contributions understand history as multi-faceted and contradictory. They reflect upon the value systems that shape material realities – land, territories, property, metropolises – to uncover the conditions of liberal social reproduction and the enduring power of colonial tropes.

Travelling across temporalities and scales, these texts brought me to my tram ride in Amsterdam. While I cannot possibly ever compare my experience to the experience of any historical actor portrayed in this reader, my anecdote aims to underline the continuity of imperial designs and their infiltration into all metrics of contemporary life. This is why an interaction that might initially seem somewhat trivial and benign, can suddenly feel so dense.

This book is divided into two parts – fiction and non-fiction – to delineate not the genre of texts themselves, but rather which structural forms the authors engage with. The first is dedicated to scholarship on literary works produced in colonial and postcolonial worlds. The latter contains historical research on material conditions of the colonised. The reader becomes a comparative exercise of reciting and recounting. If the repeated practice of racism produces race, this reader proposes reading 'again and against' to recognise the very mechanisms of its production, and how we each may be implicated in its gears. Reading 'again' is to act upon the critical perspective granted by the distance and time amongst historical moments. Reading 'against' is to challenge the sanctioned narratives that govern our liberties. Thus to understand racialisation is to also desire its deprogramming, and to release the histories of labour exploitation, gender oppression, and expropriation that it withholds.

The book begins on an island where an uncertain form lives. It's the form of Caliban, the half-human and half-monster character in William Shakespeare's *The Tempest*. For Paul Gilroy, Caliban's 'intermittent manliness' upsets what the 'human' is for the colonial enterprise.[4] For Gilroy, *The Tempest* provides an opportunity through which to understand the dynamics of race and identity – he situates the story within the realities of transatlantic slavery, with Caliban embodying the struggle against identities imposed upon him.

Sylvia Wynter's Marxist critique of the form of the novel foregrounds a similar duality; traditional literary forms often reinforce colonial ideologies, while alternative plots can challenge and redefine these structures. If the novelist's craft is connected to exchange value, Wynter proposes that resistance lies in subverting norms and disrupting dominant narratives that drive market trends. For Wynter, the plot system – 'plots' in this instance being land given to enslaved people to grow food to feed themselves – 'was, like the novel form in literature terms, the focus of resistance to the market system and market values.'[5]

Celia Britton asserts that conceptions of history are conditioned and subjective. Through the works of Parisian author Michel Butor and Martinican writer, poet, and philosopher Édouard Glissant, Britton contrasts the former's project of transparency – a 'drive towards understanding' – with the latter's operative opacity – 'the recognition of an essentially chaotic reality, an acceptance of the unknown.'[6] Opacity contests the objectifying reduction of the other, something that intelligibility prizes. Differing conceptions of one's relationship to the 'other' come into view against histories of empire in the 1950s, further illustrating the impact of colonial legacies in shaping prevalent cultural narratives.

Through the work of Portuguese author António Lobo Antunes, Luís Madureira explores the misalignments between preconception – romanticised colonial designs – and perception – their violent practices. Madureira recognises Antunes' war novels – set during and in the aftermath of the Portuguese Colonial War in Africa 1961–74 – as distinct from the works of his metropolitan peers through its rejection of universality. For Madureira, there is no redemption in Antunes's books. His writing tries 'in effect to track the waning currency of the West's notorious long narrative, to chronicle its reiterated failures to accomplish the enlightenment project of emancipation.'[7]

Despite spanning four distinct geopolitical contexts, these examples narrate the inversion of a modernist Eurocentric trope – that of being the locus of liberal social progress. These accounts evince the birth of 'progress' at the colonial margins. A 'progress' spurred by practices that spoke of 'the human' in dissenting ways. Underscoring their critique, is a recognition of fiction's ability to overturn colonial scripts and expose gross power imbalances.

The second half of the reader returns again to an island. Beginning in Trinidad in the early 1800s, Lisa Lowe foregrounds Chinese indentured labour to explore historical hierarchies of freedom and the 'liberal self'. With a focus on the autobiography of Olaudah Equiano, a formerly enslaved abolitionist, Lowe examines the autobiographical genre as a form of political expression tied to the intersecting political and economic interests of the 18th and 19th centuries. Thinking through the ideological undercurrents of said interests, Lowe reveals how 'liberal freedom has often involved the burial of the more complex currents of "new world history" upon which that freedom rests.'[8]

Colonial regimes level affirmation and forgetting to turn fiction into law, and law into practice. Muriam Haleh Davis reveals the pivotal role of colonial fictions within settler economies. She uncovers how the notion of a "Mediterranean race", a tripartite creation of settlers in California, Algeria and Israel, drove the large-scale production of citrus in these regions.

What lies at the heart of one's identity is not merely conceptual. There are material stakes – land, food, work – vulnerable to fluctuations that shape political agency or the lack thereof. Silvia Federici points to this in her survey of women's relationship to land through practices of subsistence farming. Mostly carried out by women, across a range of cultural geographies, subsistence farming contributed greatly to liberation movements throughout regions of the colonised world. Federici stresses how women's struggles for land 'have been the main opponents of the neo-liberal demand that 'market prices' determine who should live and who should die.'[9]

Drawing upon theories of labour and capital to explore the intersections of race and real estate, Brenna Bhandar and Alberto Toscano articulate how capitalist property relations preserve and rely upon values maintained by systemic inequalities. The structures of colonisation and slavery that their arguments address, weigh heavily on Black and Indigenous property owners within an American capitalist social order. 'The ideology of ownership,' Bhandar/Toscano write, 'embraced by these particular groups of people and individual landowners was mediated through histories of dispossession and displacement.'[10]

Colonial projects led to formations of empire that still serve their extractive forces today. Race, labour, and place are not inherent features of an individual, but rather conditions set by a system powered by encroachment and extraction. Hence, this book consciously straddles fiction and non-fiction; it journeys through realities-turned-fiction and fiction-turned-realities to disprove and discredit imperial fantasies.

To many who have felt the insidious effects of empire, the instinct to treat power with ambivalence can also inspire ways to defy its grip – ways that are at the very least provocative, if not outright offensive ripostes. As Sylvia Wynter contends, it is only when society rises up 'in rebellion against its external authors and manipulators that our prolonged fiction becomes temporary fact.'[11]

The tram was nearing the end of its line. The carriage was empty.

I was preparing to get off when the conductor approached me, once again unannounced. He brought up what happened earlier, brushing it off as silly banter.

But I was having none of it. 'What if I told you what you did was racist?' I asked.

His amused grin vanished immediately. His body stiffened and he spurned me, accusing me of being no fun, that I didn't know how to take a joke, that my mind was 'dark'.

Such is the darkness of interruption.

We can't attempt interruptions, we simply do.

This book stays interrupted. It rejects moralising views on identity. It does away with diasporic exceptionalisms. It chooses to stand its ground and cross-examines imperial History for what it is: a story of gaps, digressions, elisions, and suspensions.

1 Karen E. Fields and Barbara J. Fields, *Racecraft: the Soul of Inequality in American Life*. (Verso Books, 2012), 23.

2 Fields and Fields, *Racecraft*, 18.

3 Karen E. Fields and Barbara J. Fields, "Beyond 'Race Relations'" interview by Daniel Denvir, *Jacobin*, January 17, 2017, https://jacobin.com/2018/01/race-craft-racism-barbara-karen-fields.

4 Paul Gilroy "Lecture I: Suffering and Infrahumanity," in *The Tanner Lectures on Human Values*, 34, ed. Mark Matheson. (University of Utah Press, 2016), 29.

5 Sylvia Wynter, "Novel and History, Plot and Plantation," *Savacou 5*, no. 1 (1971): 99.

6 Celia Britton, "Opacity and Transparence: Conceptions of History and Cultural Difference in The Work of Michel Butor and Édouard Glissant," *French studies* 49 (1995): 310.

7 Luís Madureira, "A Supplement to the White Man's Burden: Lobo Antunes, History, the Colonial Wars, and the April Revolution," in *Facts and Fictions of António Lobo Antunes*, ed. Victor K. Mendes. (Tagus Press, 2011), 243.

8 Lisa Lowe, "Autobiography Out of Empire" in *The Intimacies of Four Continents*. (Duke University Press, 2015), 102.

9 Silvia Federici, "Women, Land-Struggles and The Valorization of Labor," *The Commoner* 10, (2005): 222

10 Brenna Bhandar and Alberto Toscano, "Race, real estate and real abstraction," *Radical Philosophy* 194 (2015): 14.

11 Wynter, "Novel and History, Plot and Plantation," 95.

FICTION

Excerpt from

Lecture I. Suffering and Infrahumanity

Paul Gilroy

in *The Tanner Lecture on Human Values*, 34: 29–38. Salt Lake City: University of Utah Press, 2016. Originally delivered at Yale University, February 21, 2014.

I sit with Shakespeare and he winces not

The freckled figure of poor hagborn Caliban, "a salvage and deformed slave,"[1] honoured Sycorax's island with a human *shape*. He has furnished many black Atlantic thinkers with a suitable beginning for their investigations into the history of racial thought. Even if we query the comforting suggestion that mere exposure to Shakespeare's art introduces us to the possibility of being human in new ways, it might be useful to return to the moment when *The Tempest*'s low characters first stumble upon the disgruntled islander. On the way to initiating their doomed conspiracy against Prospero's command, Trinculo and Stephano effect uncertainty as to exactly *what* Caliban might be. Their comic hesitancy suggests that—even as it struggled imaginatively to free itself from its Mediterranean antecedents –the distinctive ecology of the emergent Atlantic provided a unique location from which distinctively modern problems of political ontology and political anatomy would be considered. There may have been more to being human than simply having a human *shape*.

However those motley conspirators may have corresponded to their author's historical circumstances and the wealth of colonial examples familiar to his audience,[2] their confused assessment of Caliban prefigures later critical disputes. Is he to be judged a man, a monster, or, in the newly coined colonial idiom, a hybrid to be placed between the human and the animal under the sign of savagery? How might his intermittent manliness—his flickering humanity—have been modified by the bountiful, tropical circumstances in which it grew? Can the kind of thing he is possibly be connected to other menacing natural phenomena, like the strange, monstrous fish found in Caribbean waters? These speculations make that island adventure an especially good point from which to start exploring the issues that arise with the entanglement of the human and the infrahuman in the modern mesh of racial thought.

It would be an understatement to say that Caliban became an important figure for many later commentators on colonialism and decolonization. The character provided a means not only to explore the mentalities generated by the colonial project but to open up the issue of its morality and to interrogate its claims to be legitimate. George Lamming insisted that Caliban was "at once a landscape and a human situation."[3] Building upon his insight, I will suggest that race would provide those novel elements—environment and organism—with a potent articulating principle. However we classify Caliban's own motives, like Othello's, whose peri-African geography he shares, it is the idea of racial difference that makes both his alterity and his rage intelligible.

We know that Shakespeare was well acquainted with Floro, the translator into English of Montaigne's *Essays*, which had been published in 1603.[4] Gonzalo, the bard's token representative of Renaissance humanism, can be read not only as glossing passages from the essay on cannibals but also as contributing to the gradual overwriting and repudiation of its insights in favor of the bitter binary we will eventually come to know as "Manichaeism delirium."[5] Charles Taylor points out that "the figure of Caliban has been held to epitomize [a] crushing portrait of contempt of New World Aboriginals."[6] We should add the amalgamated offspring of Atlantic racial slavery to that nascent inventory.

A second motif that will be important as we trace this problem arises from the chastisement of the plotters at the end of act 4. They are victims of an assault by dogs that stands out not only as disproportionate to the threat the conspirators embody but also as a colonial motif connecting this mythic location to the practical deployment of cynegetic power that had rewritten the practice of warfare.[7] Prospero's dominion encompasses that option alongside the pastoral power that underpinned his restoration. Dogs provide not just another violent means by which the plotters are made to suffer but the favored technology for hunting them and reducing them to what they ought already to have been: servile, compliant, and ready to labor.

Just a few years later, the same issues would be clarified further in events transpiring in another, adjacent, colonial topos: the Lockean utopia provided by Robinson Crusoe's island kingdom. The assembling of anthropological categories and hierarchies would be resumed in that tamer landscape where sorcerer colonialism had been modified by the application of a severe governmental rationality that combined readily with an awe-inducing deployment of firepower.[8]

After the central questions of sovereignty and just war have been revisited and settled, temporarily at least, the relationship of these emergent systems of knowledge and the colonial fantasies they support to recognizably racial schemata would be determined in a historic colonial setting shaped by the twin practical tasks of improvement and security.

An older understanding of alterity based primarily upon categories of faith and religious practice as indexes of cultural distance was being left behind. It gave way to the new habits required by belligerent expansion. They would orbit around the polarized opposition of black to white, an arrangement that was compatible with the writings of John Locke, "the last major philosopher to seek a justification for absolute and perpetual slavery,"[9] and his successors—all more or less comfortable with the fateful association of infrahuman blackness with stupidity.[10]

An English way of thinking

Regrettably, the Nazi jurist Carl Schmitt remains our best guide to many of the most important issues that link this literature and period to our own. For reasons that are difficult to separate from his own political outlook, he identified theories of the colonial nomos as involving a "typically English" way of thinking.[11] Initially, they had been articulated by Locke, who drew upon the archive of natural law theory (mainly Roman in origin) with which the European appropriation of American land was being justified in the earliest phases of expansion.

Slavery was intrinsic to the process whereby national statecraft entered into the practice of colonial administration. This was evident in Locke's work not only in the texts that have attracted the attention of historians of raciology but in others as well, such as *Two Treatises on Government*, which is more conventionally associated with the history of liberalism than the machinations of colonial rule—an oversight that is gradually being corrected by voices from several disciplines with differing investments in the possibility of postcolonial critique.

In *Two Treatises*, we can discover the arguments that, according to Schmitt, instantiated a constitutively modern spatial ordering of the earth. The drawing of global lines was, of course, earlier, and the seeds of European planetary consciousness had grown from a series of quarrels with ancient wisdom. The New World provided a stimulus for labor theories of value, and it would become firmly and formally divided off from the proper domain of European public law. It also provided a place where something like the true state of nature could be observed. Anthropological speculations concerning the transition from natural to social and historical life were thereby entangled with the difficult, brutal work of colonial domination.

This new nomos can be distinguished by the enduring double standard to which it gave rise: a device that was exemplified in the absolutely different implications of Locke's revolutionary thinking for the colonies and the metropoles. That double standard began to enframe and even to define the unfolding of European empires. Peace and law would dwell inside their borders—which would increasingly be drawn on a planetary scale—while the chaos and conflict that Marx would later name "wild justice" reigned, catastrophically, outside. Indeed, as Europe's planetary consciousness developed, the former would become conditional upon the latter.

Many aboriginals had been disinclined to consider land as private property or to pursue English specifications for the obligation to improve it.[12] All of them fell victim to what Grégoire Chamayou usefully identifies as cynegetic authority. The novel arrangements wrought by the order of racial difference and the imperatives of accumulation alike would also be implicated in the process of enclosing common land inside the British Isles. The infrahuman composite of Caliban becomes useful again because he helps to anchor these developments in the expropriation of colonial peoples that began with the Irish.

Anthropology started to surpass and qualify the dynamics of faith that had produced otherness under the manifestos of evil rather than the natural history of primitivity. The dangers represented by the savage were shifted out of the realm of nature and assembled instead as a new variety of risk. Even in an emphatically Christian geography, they were no longer intelligible as a wholly religious phenomenon but started to become what we should now risk the accusation of "political correctness" to identify as a racial one.

We should note the intersection of empiricism and rationalism with regard to the idea of race, particularly after it had meshed with the sovereign power of the national state.[13] That confluence can be clarified further by considering a pivotal moment in *Robinson Crusoe*, the text that more than any other dramatized and affirmed industry, rationality, and improvement as the core elements of the revolutionary, self-emancipating agency of the European bourgeoisie at home and abroad.

Defoe's novel of realism and individualism was published in 1719, and, like many of its author's other works, it contributes greatly to our understanding of the economic, juridical, and military transformation that was under way in the aftermath of the Treaty of Utrecht. Crusoe hesitates to intervene violently in the life of the odious natives and is moved to deploy his superior weaponry only after he responds to the variety of kinship introduced by the prospect of an urgent operation to rescue a hostage.

By that critical point, Crusoe, who, we should also remember, has himself suffered the indignity of being a slave as well as undergone the unsettling modern experience of selling one in dubious circumstances, is perplexed by having to calculate precisely what might count as a just war against the "naked and unarmed wretches" whom his Protestant God must surely have ordained in their stupidity and savagery. He has denounced the Catholic Spanish as cruel and evil. Later, as part of pained reflections that communicate the end of the earlier pattern of responses to alterity, he will make it clear that he would rather fall into the hands of the Caribbean's cannibal savages and be devoured alive than captured by the "merciless claws of the priests and be carry'd into the Inquisition." However, as the racializing power of the colonial nomos comes more fully into play, he is at first horrified and then moved to ruthless action by the realization that the unruly natives' next feast will comprise a "white bearded man....I saw plainly by my glass a white man who lay upon the beach of the sea, with his hands and feet tyd, with flags, or things like rushes; and that he was European, and had cloaths on."[14] The problems of racial hierarchy introduced in this tableau cannot be contained in any narrow genealogy of barbarism. They should be presented in ways that make them constitutive of a revised modernity considered on its proper geopolitical compass. As the divine warrants for inequality decayed into the need to represent and account for injustice in rational terms, a new emphasis was placed upon the possibility that the human species was not, after all, unified.

Defoe had read the work of William Petty long before he wrote the book.[15] His familiarity with it provides encouragement to approach Robinson's parrot companion as a residue of preanthropological thinking in the novel. We can speculate that the brightly feathered icon of the tropics functions as a sly acknowledgment of Petty's famous speculations about human origins. Petty is remembered today as a polymath and early advocate of political arithmetic who had served as Oliver Cromwell's surveyor during the subordination of Ireland and initiated ethnographic and demographic inquiries into "the nature of the Indians of Pennsylvania" in 1686.

It is disappointing that those who write about Petty's place in the development of economics and statistics are not usually interested in his significance as an early theorist of racial difference, while those who address his innovative contribution to the history of racial thought tend not to be engaged by his submission to the seventeenth-century transformation of the arts of government.

Petty's discourse on what he called the scale of creatures featured the parrot species as a notable contender for the important position closest to man. It was immediately followed by the first English statement of what would become the fundamental principle of racialized rule. He uproots the Christian theology of mankind's unity and connects natural difference—phenotypical variation—to a color-coded hierarchy specified with precision in the open space between the notions of race and species.

> That of man it selfe there seems to be severall species, To say nothing of Gyants and Pigmies or of that sort of small men who have little speech and feed chiefly upon fish...for of these sorts of men, I venture to say nothing, but that 'tis very possible there may be Races and generations of such since we know that there are men of 7 foot high and others but 4 foot....I say there may be races and Generations of such men whereof we know the Individualls...there be others (differences) more considerable, that is, between the Guiny Negroes & the Middle Europeans; & of Negroes between those of Guiny and those who live about the Cape of Good Hope, which last are the Most beastlike of all the Souls (?Sorts) of Men whith whom our Travellers arre well acquainted. I say that the Europeans do not only differ from the aforementioned Africans in Collour...but also...in Naturall Manners, & in the internall Qualities of their Minds.[16]

It is unsurprising that Petty's commentary on the division and stratification of humankind was shot through with elaborate observations on every different variety of living creature. The novel relationship he proposed between observable differences, cognitive capacity, and the natural constitution of humans was part of the gradual shift from race as static taxonomy to race as a matter of historical lineage.

To cut that very long story short, a secularized dualism arose to manage the distinction between the mental and the physical over the wreckage of the split between soul and body. The Negro gradually became a primary object of anatomo-political inquiry and was judged to have been rendered by nature both intellectually inferior and physically distinctive. At that point in the eighteenth century, the black body did not yet disclose its fundamental difference through the fixed idiom of a new racial semiosis. How the body would communicate those aesthetic and scientific truths had not yet been settled.

The inferiority of Negroes was conveyed above all by the skin, which no less of an authority than Kant informed his readers could resist the normal tools and techniques of chastisement. But the body affords many possible points of entry into what was also a heavily gendered discourse.[17] It concerned not just the skulls we know so well, but a whole crop of unlikely bodily markers: beards and pelvises as well as breasts would supply alternative indexes of a difference that articulated science and aesthetics. Amid all of them, the Negro's relatively impenetrable hide should concern us for what it reveals—or conceals—about the uneven distribution of humanity in a world where race and slavery have been tightly associated. Their mutual connection underpinned the transformation of human beings into brutes—objects differentiated by the fact that their suffering was of no consequence either for the calculus of capital accumulation or for the ethics of mercy, sympathy, and pity.

The word *brute* can refer both to animals and to humans, but it is important that we do not place these infrahuman figures too neatly between those poles, as if they occupied a settled intermediate place in a rigid scale where "Caucasian" man appears at the top and animal life is ranged below. The geometry involved in locating infrahumanity has always been more complex, as Petty's employment of two distinct but intersecting lists of creatures had shown. That arrangement manifests not the ultimate unity of all varieties of life but a complex gradation of the human configured so that some kinds of people are closer to nature than others whose more highly valued lives are endowed with a variety of historicality that guarantees their dominance and superiority.

Today, what styles itself as posthumanism has created some standard responses to this unsavory history. Opposition to racism is generally and wrongly taken for granted by almost all of them. That silence is a well-intentioned but deeply problematic gesture that allows or requires consideration of the specific attributes of antiracist politics to be set aside. For reasons that are not altogether clear, interspecies conflict then recedes in the face of increased concern with intraspecies relations.

The influential work of Donna Haraway is paradigmatic of the plea to employ interaction with our companion species as a mechanism to learn the transferable skills involved in "living intersectionally." Certainly, not all feminist commentary on these matters follows her into contempt for past humanism or lapses into a simplistic presentation of it *only* as a source of racism rather than a complex response to the pathologies that racism creates: "The discursive tie between the colonized, the enslaved, the noncitizen, and the animal—all reduced to type, all Others to rational man, and all essential to his bright constitution—is at the heart of racism and flourishes, lethally, in the entrails of humanism."[18]

Human exceptionalism has underpinned the impending disaster that can be gauged in the looming catastrophe of the Anthropocene or, more accurately, the Capitalocene. Apparently, there is liberation in the prospect of human beings recognizing themselves as just one more "critter" among many. Though we may share a commitment to radical relationality and a political ecology that refuses the conceits of approaching nature as an exploitable, limitless resource, those who speak in the modern tradition defined by struggles against racialized confinement within the natural order can be expected to have less enthusiasm for this way of proceeding. We agree that the human-animal intersection that has been explored so extensively is significant for the life of biopolitical categories in general and racial nominalism in particular. However, that commitment should not encourage us to submerge the origins of racism in a generic problem that can too conveniently be labeled humanism.

The slave, the Negro, and the indigene experience enforced association with the animal. For them, the liberatory and solidary possibilities released by the process of "becoming animal" are less appealing precisely because they are almost entirely animal already. Perhaps that is why, in the tradition of critical analysis and interpretation that has been shaped by the wounds of slavery and colonial conquest, the refiguration of the human and the critique of humanism have often been responses made to the issues of racial alienation and racial hierarchy.

Some of the most interesting responses to these historic problems reside in discussions of the work of Franz Kafka, who, more than any other writer, placed the human, the infrahuman, and the animal in disturbing relation in order to establish a variety of modernism "far away from the continent of Man."[19] Similar debate has also arisen around the writing of those whom Kafka inspired, particularly J. M. Coetzee, who, writing from South Africa, the one place in the whole world where the immediate salience of racial categories to political life could not be forsworn, offered a number of insights into developing an ethics of alterity capable of connecting the suffering of animals to the suffering visited on human beings in the name of racial hygiene and hierarchy. Often, those who engage Coetzee's work for its ethical stimulation pass swiftly over the fundamental question of the damage to humanity and democracy that has derived from South Africa's unexpectedly resilient racial order.[20]

These racial problems of human, infrahuman, and animal life have surfaced repeatedly in the black Atlantic archive and merit extensive investigation. Petrified by what he called the "inhuman detail" involved in devising spectacular and exotic torments for the slaves of Surinam, John Gabriel Stedman vividly reported the case of Cadetty, a slave punished by being lodged in a dog's kennel from which he was required to bark at each boat passing on the nearby river.[21] The slave-catching capacities of the fila brasileiro are, of course, legendary, and Frederick Douglass is the best known of many slave writers to have placed slave and animal lives in relation, in particular chronicling the role of dogs in tracking runaways.[22] William Wells Brown, who delighted his readers with the tale of a slavehunting parson who imported his vicious hounds from specialist Cuban breeders, devotes almost a whole chapter of *Clotel* to the role of dogs in "The Negro Chase." Henry Bibb was hunted by dogs, and Solomon Northup repeated what would become the standard script on the abilities of the hounds that had been bred to catch runaways: "The dogs used on Bayou Boeuf for hunting slaves are a kind of blood-hound but a far more savage breed than is found in the Northern States. They will attack a negro at their master's bidding and cling to him as the common bulldog will cling to a four footed animal."[23]

The lengthy chronicle of bloodhounds and hellhounds arrives eventually at the Chicago animal laboratory where Richard Wright was employed to assist in cutting the vocal cords of dogs in order to prevent them from disturbing patients elsewhere in the hospital. That disturbing tale was worth repeating in two different publications, one autobiographical, one fictional: "The hospital kept us four Negroes as though we were close kin to the animals we tended, huddled together down in the underworld corridors of the hospital, separated by a vast psychological distance...just as America had kept us locked in the dark underworld of American life for three hundred years."[24]

1 *The Tempest*, 1.2.2 81–84.

2 Ronald Takaki, "*The Tempest* in the Wilderness: The Racialization of Savagery," *Journal of American History* 79, no. 3 (1992): 892–912; Rob Nixon, "Caribbean and African Appropriations of *The Tempest*," *Critical Inquiry* 13, no. 3 (1987): 557–78.

3 George Lamming, *Pleasures of Exile* (1960; reprint, London: Allison and Busby, 1984), 118.

4 Roberto Fernández Retamar et al., "Caliban: Notes towards a Discussion of Culture in Our America," *Massachusetts Review* 15, nos. 1–2 (1974): 7–72.

5 Frantz Fanon, *The Wretched of the Earth*, translated by Constance Farrington (New York: Grove Press, 1963), 141.

6 Charles Taylor, *Multiculturalism and the Politics of Recognition* (Princeton, NJ: Princeton University Press, 1992), 26.

7 Grégoire Chamayou, *Manhunts: A Philosophical History* (Princeton, NJ: Princeton University Press, 2012), chap. I; Tzetan Todorov, *The Conquest of America*, translated by Richard Howard (New York: Harper and Row, 1984), chap. 3.

8 Peter Hulme, *Colonial Encounters: Europe and the Native Caribbean, 1492–1797* (London: Methuen, 1986), chap. 5.

9 David B. Davis, *The Problem of Slavery in the Age of Revolution, 1770–1823* (Ithaca, NY: Cornell University Press, 1975), 45.

10 See Ronald A. T. Judy, *Disforming the American Canon: African Arabic Slave Narratives and the Vernacular* (Minneapolis: University of Minnesota Press, 1993), chap. 4.

11 Carl Schmitt, *The Nomos of the Earth: In the International Law of the Jus Publicum Europaeum*, translated by G. L. Ulmen (New York: Telos Press, 2003), 98.

12 Peter Hulme, "The Hidden Hand of Nature," in *Enlightenment and Its Shadows*, edited by Peter Hulme and Ludmilla Jordanova (London: Routledge, 1990).

13 David Theo Goldberg, *The Racial State* (Oxford: Blackwell, 2002).

14 Daniel Defoe, *Robinson Crusoe* (Harmondsworth: Penguin, 1965), 233.

15 William Petty is mentioned in chapter 8 of Defoe's *An Essay upon Projects* (1697).

16 Rhodri Lewis, ed., *William Petty on the Order of Nature: An Unpublished Manuscript Treatise* (Tempe: Arizona Center for Medieval and Renaissance Studies, 2012), 122.

17 Londa Schiebinger, *Nature's Body* (Boston: Beacon Press, 1993).

18 Donna Haraway, *When Species Meet* (Minneapolis: University of Minnesota Press, 2008), 18

19 Walter Benjamin, *Illuminations*, translated by Harry Zohn, edited by Hannah Arendt (London: Fontana, 1973), 122.

20 An important exception to this is Cynthia Willett's essay "Ground Zero for a Post-moral Ethics in J. M. Coetzee's *Disgrace* and Julia Kristeva's Melancholic," *Continental Philosophy Review* 45, no. I (2012): 1–22.

21 John Gabriel Stedman, *Narrative, of a Five Years' Expedition, against the Revolted Negroes of Surinam* (London: J. Johnson and Th. Payne, 1813), 1:350.

22 "They are hunted with dogs, kept for the purpose, and regularly trained. Enmity is Instilled into the blood-hounds by these means: A master causes a slave to tie up the dog and beat it unmercifully. He then sends the slave away and bids him climb a tree; after which he unties the dog, puts him upon the track of the man and encourages him to pursue it until he discovers the slave. Sometimes, in hunting the negroes, if the owners are not present to call off the dogs, the slaves are torn in pieces—(sensation); this has often occurred." Frederick Douglass, "The Horrors of Slavery and England's Duty to Free the Bondsman: An Address Delivered in Taunton, England, on September 1, 1846," *Somerset County Gazette*, September 5, 1846; John Blassingame et al., eds., *The Frederick Douglass Papers*, ser. I, *Speeches, Debates, and Interviews* (New Haven, CT: Yale University Press, 1979), 1:371.

23 Gilbert Osofsky, ed., *Puttin' on Ole Massa* (New York: Harpers, 1969), 305.

24 Richard Wright, *American Hunger* (London: Gollancz, 1978), 59.

Novel and History, Plot and Plantation

Sylvia Wynter

in *We Must Learn to Sit Down Together and Talk about a Little Culture: Decolonising Essays, 1967–1984*, Peepal Tree Press, 2022.

First let us define our terms. What, in our context, is the novel? What, in our context, is history? What *is* our context? George Beckford, a Jamaican economist writes:

> In America, the *locus* of the plantation system is the Caribbean. Indeed, this region is generally regarded as *the* classic plantation area. So much so that social anthropologists have described the region as a culture sphere, labelled Plantation America.[1]

The Caribbean area is the classic plantation area since many of its units were "planted" with people, not in order to form societies, but to carry on plantations whose aim was to produce single crops for the market. That is to say, the plantation-societies of the Caribbean came into being as adjuncts to the market system; their peoples came into being as an adjunct to the product, to the single crop commodity – the sugar cane – which they produced. As Eric Williams has shown, our societies were both cause and effect of the emergence of the market economy; an emergence which marked a change of such world historical magnitude, that we are all, without exception still "enchanted", imprisoned, deformed and schizophrenic in its bewitched reality.

Now, the novel form itself, according to Goldmann, came into being with the extension and dominance of the market economy, and "appears to us to be in effect, the transposition on the literary plane, of the daily life within an individualist society, born of production for the market."[2] The novel form and our societies are twin children of the same parents. No wonder Miguel Ángel Asturias, a Plantation novelist of a Plantation Republic, Guatemala, wrote in unbelieving despair, after the C.I.A.-backed overthrow of the legally elected Government of Árbenz: "These things that happen? …It's best to call them fiction!"[3] History, then, these things that happen, is, in the plantation context, itself fiction; a fiction written, dominated, controlled by forces external to itself. It is clear then, that it is only when the society, or elements of the society rise up in rebellion against its external authors and manipulators that our prolonged fiction becomes temporary fact. The novel *New Day* shows not one, but two of these historical collisions and links them, suggesting in fiction their factual connection.

The epic form, Lukács remarks, knows nothing of questions. The hero is essentially at one with the values of his world. With the novel form, the rupture of the hero and the now inauthentic values of his world begins. The novel form is in essence a question mark.[4]

In *New Day*, the second, and younger hero, the hero whom we can term the "positive hero" as distinct from Davie, the earlier and "problematic hero" asks his great uncle, the narrator, a question which is crucial to the novel and to our discussion.

> Tell me Uncle John. You have spoken of the old things, but you have never given me an opinion. We have been taught in our history classes that Gordon and Bogle were devils, while Eyre was a saint who only did what he did because it was necessary. You knew both Gordon and Bogle. Were they as bad as they were painted?[5]

The old man's answer is evasive and ambivalent. It is part and parcel of the evasive ambivalence of the "ideology" of gradualism which was the ideology of the more idealistic middle-class movement summed up in the People's National Party, a party which emerged after the upheavals of the Jamaican people in 1938. In fact, it is clear that Garth himself is a thinly disguised portrait of Norman Washington Manley. On the negative side, one could dismiss this movement, as Ken Post does,[6] by calling it merely the "middle-class backlash" against the threatened takeover by varied and manifold popular forces. But in the context of plantation societies like ours, the usual terms cannot be applied without examination

To evaluate the old man's answer, we must examine the basic significance of the question. The question he is asked is one of historical fact. Yet, from the way Garth asks the question we see that the history taught in the schools is a history based around a Manichean myth. Bogle and Gordon are devils. Eyre is a saint. This was the version of history taught by the forces that upheld the plantation. And the forces that upheld the plantation were the forces of the market. These forces, the forces of the *emporium* (*emporio*) (to borrow Asturias's pun) are the forces of the *imperio* – the Empire. The emporialist forces and the imperialist forces are one.

Bogle, Gordon and Eyre are personalities, figures caught in a clash and conflict that are not even primarily of their making. For they are caught in a collision and a clash that was inherent and inbuilt, and still is, between the plantation system, a system, owned and dominated by external forces, and what we shall call the plot system, the indigenous, autochthonous system. Miguel Ángel Asturias defines this clash as the struggle between, "…the indigenous peasant who accepts that corn should be sown only as food, and the *creole* who sows it as a business, burning down forests of precious trees, impoverishing the earth in order to enrich himself".[7]

Basically then this is a struggle between the indigenous man still involved in a world of what Marx terms *use-value*, where a product is made in response to a human need; and the market economy world with its structure of *exchange-value* where the product is made in response to its profitability in the market. In the world of use-value, human needs dominate the product. In the world of exchange-value, the product, the thing made, dominates, manipulates human need.

Now, as Goldmann argues, the novel form is, "among all literary forms, the most immediately and directly linked to the economic structures in the narrow sense of the term, to the structure of exchange and production for the market."[8] But because the writer, the artist, is by the very nature of his craft linked to the structure of use-value statements, the impulse of creation thus being directed by human needs, he remained as a hangover in the new form of societies. The novel form reflects his critical and oppositional stance to a process of alienation which had begun to fragment the very human community, without which the writer has neither purpose, nor source material, nor view of the world, nor audience. The novel form, a product of the market economy, its exchange structure – its individual here set free to realise his individuality by the "liberal" values of individualism, linked to the very existence of the market system – nevertheless, instead of expressing the values of the market society, develops and expands as a form of resistance to this very market society. In effect, the novel form and the novel is the critique of the very historical process which has brought it to such heights of fulfilment.

V.S. Naipaul's *A House for Mr. Biswas*, whilst it celebrates the talent of its author, and awards him a recognised place among the elite world, is nevertheless a profound indictment of a deprived world in which, to realise his being, Biswas must alienate himself from an impossible community, distorted by phantasmagoric circumstance, to shelter in a jerry-built house and a Prefect car. The individual, dreamt of in the liberal market economy as being now totally sovereign and free, is shipwrecked by the later developments of this structure which prohibits his fulfilment and leaves him huddled in a house, escaping from civilisation; a Robinson Crusoe clinging to his island for survival through escape from the outside world. His victory, like ours, is pyrrhic.

The "problematic hero" is the corollary of the problematic novel. This problematic hero is exemplified in Davie and, to some extent, in his father. For like Okonkwo in Chinua Achebe's *Things Fall Apart*, old father Campbell, clinging to his belief in God's order and in the inevitability of British justice, is shot down by British soldiers, defending the market economy, i.e. the plantation, against the challenge of the peasant farmers and the agro-proletarian workers. To make the world safe for the market economy, families are broken up, as in Ngugi Wa Thiong'o's, *Weep Not Child*, and indeed, in *New Day*. Hundreds are shot down. The techniques of terror which will be brought to perfection under Hitler and Stalin against Europeans, in Europe itself, are perfected in the *emporium-imperium*, plantation units. Vic Reid in *New Day* describes the actual historical fact of Colonel Hobbs, a gentleman, who grew roses up at the barracks at Newcastle, getting nine "rebels" to hang each other in a chapel at Fonthill, ordering thirteen others to dig a trench, and then having the soldiers shoot them into the mass grave. Hobbs had a problem of finding enough quicklime to sanitarily dispose of the bodies. He had another problem too. Afraid of being mocked for his natural inclination to clemency for the rebels, he felt he had to match and outdo in terror his fellow officers. He committed suicide afterwards. In Ngugi Wa Thiong'o's *Weep Not Child*, the hero confronts and is tortured by the English settler-farmer who grows pyrethrum for the market.

The reaction of the planters in 1865 to the death of a handful of the manager colon-creole class who are killed by Bogle and his followers is one of outrage, not only at the thought of bloodshed but at the threat to the plantation, which was to them the very core and seat of the structure of their "civilised" values. It is not accidental that H. G. de Lisser, a colon-creole writer who dealt with 1865 in a novel called *Revenge* sees the battle between the plantation forces and Bogle's forces as a battle between light and darkness. Bogle's followers watch anxiously for a sign from heaven, after a Cecil B. DeMille-type ritual ceremony. Joyce, the English plantation heroine, watches anxiously too, as she observes

> a great mass of black clouds… moving slowly across the sky …It seemed as though the inky mass were gaining inch by inch on the shining space [i.e. lit up by the moon] … were menacing it with an inevitable doom of obliteration; it was like a huge formless monster advancing slowly but with pitiless tread towards a thing of beauty which it had doomed to extinction…[9]

The symbolism is quite clear. This passage illustrates what Ramchand, paraphrasing from Fanon, has called "the terrified consciousness" of the Whites.[10] But I am trying to shift from the ground of race, which is but one factor in the equation, to the ground Asturias defines. Bogle's followers are men who predominantly sow for food, secondarily for the market. Thus, use-value determines their structure of values. Joyce belongs to the plantation system, the exchange structure; and "the thing of beauty" whose extinction she fears is the complex of values by which she lives; values which have their positive aspect; for example the hero shows a sense of responsibility, thoughtfulness; but values, too, which bolster their dominant and exploitative position.

Bogle's followers, according to de Lisser, cheer wildly when the black clouds cover the moon. It is a sign that they will be helped by God to purge wickedness from the land; and the white creole hero's mother is in no doubt that it is her race, class and their structure of values that are to be purged out of the land. In both De Lisser's novel and in Vic Reid's, the basic confrontation is between the plantation and the plot and the structure of values which each represents. I suggest that the conflict and clash that has taken place between two defined groups in this conference[11], between those who defend the "autonomy" of the "civilised", highly educated artist and those who defend the claims of the community and the folk, has little to do with racial division and everything to do with those who, like Joyce, defend the values of the plantation and those who, like Bogle, represent the values of the plot. Perhaps most typical of all is the "silent majority", ambivalent like *New Day*'s narrator-hero between the two. For if the history of Caribbean society is that of a dual relation between plantation and plot, the two poles which originate in a single historical process, the ambivalence between the two has been, and is, the distinguishing characteristic of the Caribbean response. This ambivalence is at once the root cause of our alienation; and the possibility of our salvation.

To explain briefly the plantation-plot dichotomy we are compelled to make generalisations.

1. Before the unique Western experience which began with the discovery of the New World, all societies of mankind existed in what Senghor describes as dual oscillatory process in which Man adapts to Nature, and adapts Nature to his own needs.

2. But with the discovery of the New World and its vast exploitable lands, that process which has been termed the "reduction of Man to Labour and of Nature to Land" had its large-scale beginning. From this moment on, Western Man saw himself as "the lord and possessor of Nature".[12] The one-way transformation of Nature began. Since man is a part of Nature, a process of dehumanisation and alienation was set in train. In old societies with traditional values based on the old relation, resistance could be put up to the dominance of the new dehumanising system. In new societies like ours, created for the market, there seemed at first to be no possibility of such a tradition.

3. But from early, the planters gave the slaves plots of land on which to grow food to feed themselves in order to maximise profits. We suggest that this plot system was, like the novel form in literature terms, the focus of resistance to the market system and market values.

4. For African peasants transplanted to the plot all the structure of values that had been created by traditional societies of Africa; the land remained the Earth – and the Earth was a goddess; man used the land to feed himself and to offer first fruits to the Earth; his funeral was the mystical reunion with the earth. Because of this traditional concept, the social order remained primary. Around the growing of yam, of food for survival, he created on the plot a folk culture – the basis of a social order – in three hundred years.

This culture recreated traditional values – use values. This folk culture became a source of cultural guerilla resistance to the plantation system.

But since he worked on the plantation and was in fact the labour, land and capital, he was ambivalent between the two. After the abolition of slavery, the slave-turned-peasant grew crops both to feed himself, and to sell on the market. The plantation, dependent on mass-labour, was determined to use their ownership of the land to compel him back to work, and to his role in the structure of exchange-value. The plantation was the superstructure of civilisation; and the plot was the roots of culture.[13] But there was a rupture between them, the superstructure was not related to its base, did not respond to the needs of the base, but rather to the demands of external shareholders and the metropolitan market. The plantation was run by the manager class, the colon class. This class and the labouring indigenous class faced each other across barricades that are inbuilt in the very system which created them. That is why the clash in 1865 and the clash in 1938 and the future clashes are unavoidable unless the system itself is transformed.

In 1865, in the historical records, the rebels as they killed Charles Price, a black building contractor, shouted back to his claim that he was black: "You are black but you have a white heart!"[14] Several white doctors were allowed to escape, unhurt. There is, as Barrington Moore points out, a logical and rational basis to peasant resistance to the market economy.[15] "A white heart" aptly describes the man whom Miguel Ángel Asturias calls "the man who sows for profit",[16] the man involved in a structure of exchange value – which is all of us. Our place in the confrontation is largely determined by whether we accept or reject this structure.

Our appreciation and revaluation of the folk is not, therefore, the heroic folkish mythology of a Hitler. For we accept folk culture as a point outside the system where the traditional values can give us a focus of criticism against the impossible reality in which we are enmeshed.

But there is no question of going back to a society, a folk pattern, whose structure has already been undermined by the pervasive market economy. Robert Serumaga shows this in *Return to the Shadows*. Joe, running away from yet another army takeover, goes home to his mother, to tie himself back to the umbilical cord. But his mother has been raped, and his young cousins raped and murdered by soldiers who are the representatives of the large central force which monopoly capitalism, with or without state intervention, must, by the logic of its existence, have at its disposal, to crush any dissent from its totalitarian power.[17] The plantation system which, under the liberal free-trade rhetoric, the rhetoric which freed the slaves, compensated the masters and set the slaves free in a world dominated by market relations, to fend naked for themselves, was the first sketch of monopoly capitalism. George William Gordon, we suggest, wheeling and dealing, buying land, speculating, owning a newspaper, acting as a produce dealer, speaking vehemently in the House of Assembly, claiming the rights of Magna Carta as a freeborn son of Jamaica, embodied the liberal rhetoric and took it seriously. When he became a threat to the emporio/imperio dominance he was hanged by the *reality* of a totalitarian monopoly system. The outcry in England was made by Liberal elements who could, in England, enjoy the freedom offered by liberal free-trade politics. But Carlyle saw clearly that plantations were made for lazy Negroes to learn the gospel of work under the spur of the whip. No one dissented when Crown Colony Government was imposed, and the Assembly discarded. The Assembly, like Gordon, was a piece of liberal rhetoric which the brute reality of the system could no longer afford. Bogle and his followers were taught a lesson – in the same way as Indian peasants rioting in Bengal in the 1860s against having to grow indigo as a commercial crop for the English had to be taught a lesson. The world had to be kept safe for the market economy.

History, to help in this task, had to be distorted. The myth of history was used by the plantation to keep its power secure. It was necessary that Gordon and Bogle should be painted "black"; and since "remembrance of things past can give rise to dangerous insights" much of the history was suppressed. As the old man in *New Day* complains:

> They do no know what we have seen, for no place has been found in their English history books for the fire that burnt us in 'Sixty Five.[18]

He tells his grandnephew Garth some of it; and this consciousness of the past and of his grandfather Davie's role in it, causes Garth to see himself as the new dedicated elite leader of the masses. But his historical apprehension will be different from theirs. For he still asks "Were they as bad as they were painted?"[19] The history he has been taught is the history of the plantation, the official history of the superstructure;

the only history which has been written. But the plot, too, has its own history. A secretive history expressed in folk songs "War down a Mona and the Queen never know, War O War O War O", and the old Anglo-Indian General Jackson hunting down the rebels in a tragicomic folksong:

> Oh General Jackson
> Oh General Jackson, you kill all the black men dem.[20]

In the Kumina ceremony, Bogle appears through an initiate as an ancestor- god. When asked in 1965 about Bogle, Morant Bay people answered about Bogle and Gordon:

> Is Justice they were seeking! Justice for the people.[21]

Again as Moore points out, there is a profound peasant sense of justice which is separate from the abstract concept of the law of the plantation. The law of the plantation is based on the rights of property. The justice of the peasant is based on the needs of the people who form the community. There is hardly an aspect in which there is not this dichotomy of attitudes. No aspect in which the attitudes and values of the dominant "colon-creole plantation structure" is not used in an essentially exploitative relation to the indigenous plot values.

The clashes of 1865 and 1938 are episodes in a historical continuum. It is significant that de Lisser sees 1865 as an isolated episode told through the personal relations of three white characters – the hero, the heroine, and the villain who joins with the black "against his race and class" in order to win Joyce, but who dies protecting her from an "unmentionable horror" in the end. The real conflict is banished and suppressed even though de Lisser senses the continuing unease in his society and writes his book as warning to the dark clouds *not* to cover the moon.

Reid on the other hand, caught up in the release of 1938 and the growth of national feeling, wrote his novel to restore the written past to a people who had only the oral past; and to the middle class who thought, as Naipaul did, that nothing was created in the West Indies and therefore there was no history. Reid wanted to prophesy the future by placing his then present in the context of an almost epic past. In the first part of his book when he deals with the problematic hero Davie who fails (he goes off to the Morant Cays and creates a community, which is broken up once his son establishes wage scales to respond to the market business of shipping bananas). But Davie died before that, having lost Lucille Dubois, his wife, through his new obsession. His quest then turns out to be in vain and finally inauthentic, as with all the great novels. He dies in a hurricane, imprisoned under the weight of a tree.

The second part of the book with its "positive" hero fails because Garth is made to bear the weight of an expectation that can never be realised. Whilst the first part of the book parallels and patterns the structure of its society, and reflects its failure to satisfy human needs, the second part fails by ignoring the fact that changes in the superstructure of the plantation – a new Constitution, even Independence – were changes which left the basic system untouched, and which only prolonged the inevitable and inbuilt confrontation between the plantation and the plot: between the city, which is the commercial expression of the plantation, and its marginal masses, disrupted from the plot; this is the conflict and the clash that we have seen reflected here in this conference, on different levels of awareness, between those who justify and defend the system; and those who challenge it.

1 George L. Beckford, "The Economics of Agricultural Resource Use and Development," *Social and Economic Studies*, vol. 18, no. 4 (December 1969): 325.

2 Lucien Goldmann, *Pour une sociologie du roman* (Paris: Éditions Gallimard, 1964), 24.

3 Miguel Ángel Asturias, *Week-end en Guatemala* (Buenos Aires: Editorial Goyanarte, 1956), title page.

4 George Lukács, *The Theory of the Novel: A Historio-Philosophical Essay on the Forms of Great Epic Literature*, trans. by Anna Bostock (1920; Cambridge, MA: MIT Press, 1977), 66.

5 V. S. Reid, *New Day* (1949; Chatham, NJ: Chatham Bookseller/Alfred Knopf, 1972), 277.

6 Ken Post's account of the 1938 worker rebellion and the middle class response is in *Arise Ye Starvelings: The Jamaican Labour Rebellion of 1938 and its Aftermath* (The Hague: Martinus Nijhoff, 1978).

7 The specific quotation could not be located but the same sentiment expressed can be found in Asturias, *Hombres de Maíz* (Buenos Aires: Editorial Losada, 1949), 13.

8 Goldmann, *Pour une sociologie*, 189.

9 H. G. de Lisser, *Revenge: A Tale of Old Jamaica* (Kingston: The Gleaner, 1919).

10 The phrase comes from chapter xiii of Kenneth Ramchand's *The West Indian Novel and Its Background* (London: Faber, 1970), 223–236.

11 The conference referred to in this essay was the Association of Commonwealth Literature and Language Studies (ACLALS) conference of 1971 at the Mona (Jamaica) campus of the University of the West Indies. At this conference, described from a participant point of view by Kamau Brathwaite in *LX: The Love Axe/l* (forthcoming), there were major clashes between political and aesthetic radicals and the "old guard" and defenders of the Creole "all o' we is one" settlement that was profoundly suspicious of the attempts to restore submerged African "folk" elements to visibility.

12 Léopold Sédar Senghor, "Le problème de la culture" in *Liberte I: Négritude et Humanismse* (Paris: Éditions du Seuil, 1964), 93.

13 The Custos Baron van Ketelhodt, one of the principal figures of 1865, defended the needs of sugar against beet, by claiming that the sugar estate was the centre of civilisation in the island.

14 The exact wording of Wynter's quote could not be located, but Gad Heuman's *The Killing Time: The Morant Bay Rebellion in Jamaica* (Knoxville: University of Tennessee Press, 1994), 9, has the quote as: "… he has got a black skin and a white heart."

15 Barrington Moore, *Social Origins of Dictatorship and Democracy: Lord and Peasant in the Making of the Modern World* (Boston: Beacon Press, 1966).

16 Miguel Àngel Asturias, *Hombres de máz* (Buenos Aires: Editorial Losada, 1949), 13.

17 Robert Serumaga, *Return to the Shadows* (London: Heinemann, 1969).

18 Reid, *New Day*, 262.

19 Ibid., 277.

20 "Oh, General Jackson" in *Jamaican Song and Story: Annancy Stories, Digging Songs, Ring Tunes and Dancing Tunes*, Walter Jekyll, collected and ed. (1907; New York: Dover Publications, Inc., 1966), 233.

21 The source of this quotation could not be located.

Opacity and Transparence

Conceptions of History and Cultural Difference in the Work of Michel Butor and Éduoard Glissant

Celia Britton

in *French Studies* 49, no. 3 (July 1, 1995): 308–20.
Unless otherwise noted excerpts translated by Louise Darblay.

Despite their very different backgrounds, the Parisian Michel Butor and the Martinican Édouard Glissant are similar figures in many respects. They both believe that literature is necessarily connected to a philosophical and political world view. In that world view, also, *history* is a central element for both writers: their novels revolve around the struggle for an awareness of oneself as the product of particular historical forces, and both see this as the only possible basis for self-knowledge and for free, coherent action in the present. *La Modification*,[1] for instance, traces the process whereby Léon Delmont gradually achieves a more authentic sense of his own identity through a realization of his situation in history; and, in similar terms, the hero of Glissant's *Le Quatrième Siècle*[2] exclaims: 'Le passé. Qu'est le passé sinon la connaissance qui te roidit dans la terre et te pousse en foule dans demain?' (p. 280).[1]

Secondly, Butor and Glissant both have a very strong sense of *place*: the qualitative specificity of individual places (as the title of Butor's *Le Génie du lieu*[3] series suggests), and also topographical relations within and between them. *L'Emploi du temps*[4] is taken up with Revel's mapping of the city of Bleston; the same fascination with the complexity of urban space can be seen in the descriptions of Rome and Paris in *La Modification* and

1 'The past. What is the past if not the knowledge that anchors you to the ground and propels you into tomorrow?'

Degrés;[5] and *Mobile*[6] does the same thing on the much vaster scale of the United States as a whole. For Glissant, the landscape of the tiny island of Martinique is a constant and deeply emotional reality: 'moi qui en quelques pas puis en faire le tour, et qui jamais ne peux l'épuiser' ('Poétique et inconscient martiniquais', p. 237).[7] [II] But it is equally Martinique's relation to other places that has to be established and clarified: to Africa, to France, and to the other islands in the Caribbean — 'Un pays d'île ne se trouve pas, s'il n'y a pas d'autres îles' (*Mahagony*, p. 220).[8] [III]

II 'I, who can walk around it in just a few steps, yet can never exhaust it'

III 'An island country cannot truly exist, if there are no other islands'

Glissant sees the landscape as inseparable from its history — 'Notre paysage est son propre monument ... C'est tout histoire' (*Le Discours antillais*, p. 21)[9] [IV] — and as a mode of access to that history: the mahogany tree whose description opens *Mahagony* simultaneously stands for the history and the topography of the island: 'Un arbre est tout un pays, et si nous demandons quel est ce pays, aussitôt nous plongeons à l'obscur indéracinable du temps, que nous peinons à débroussailler ...' (*Mahagony*, p. 13).[V] Butor is less explicit about this equation, but the cities in his novels are nevertheless represented as the sedimentation of layers of history — classical Rome followed by Catholic Rome and then Fascist Rome in *La Modification*, for instance. Thus for both authors, places are constituted by their histories. Moreover, different places have, not only different histories, but different conceptions of what history is.

IV 'Our landscape is its own monument ... It is all history' (Édouard Glissant, *Caribbean Discourse: Selected Essays*, translated by J. Michael Dash, University Press of Virginia, 1989, p. 11)

V 'A tree is an entire country, and when we ask what this country is, we suddenly plunge into the obscure, unfathomable roots of time, through which we struggle to clear a path...'

As this implies, both Butor and Glissant are concerned with cultural difference. How do we, as individuals and as communities, relate to what is socially and culturally *other*? Central to this is the critique of colonialism and racism, which underpins all Glissant's writing and which in Butor's case gradually — from *L'Emploi du temps* through *Degrés* and *Mobile* — becomes a major issue. But the question is posed more generally as well: in *Mobile* the other is America as a whole; in *L'Emploi du temps* it is the north of England (which Butor himself experienced as far more alien and difficult than Egypt);[10] in Glissant's novels, it is as much Africa as France.

All these relationships between different communities are seen, more or less explicitly by both authors, as historically determined. But their work also shows how the link between history and cultural difference involves a more subjective dimension as well, in that the individual's attitude towards the phenomenon of difference is conditioned, if not very consciously, by his or her *conception* of history. In other words, since my sense of my own identity is crucially dependent upon my sense of my community's history, my relationship to the other is also constituted on that basis. It follows therefore that Butor's and Glissant's conception of the relation to the other should be significantly different. Here the similarities that I have outlined give way to marked divergences;

and my argument here will be that these can be traced back to their different sense of history.

Throughout the work of both writers we find a striking opposition between *transparence* and *opacity* — but they attribute opposite values to the two terms. Butor's writing is governed overall by a very general drive towards *understanding*. This means achieving transparence: the supreme values are consciousness, lucidity, and illumination. Understanding cultural difference is one case of this, and it produces the same imagery: Revel's initial reaction to Bleston's otherness presents it as impossible to understand *because* dark, foggy, dirty and opaque; he refers to 'ce mur de verre trouble qui me séparait de la ville' (p. 52).[VI] His aim is to turn Bleston into transparence and intelligibility — like the detective figure who 'transforme la réalité, la purifie par la seule puissance de sa vision perçante et juste' (p. 147) [VII] — and the city's opacity does indeed yield to this gradual penetration: by the penultimate chapter, Jacques finds that 'cette ville, je l'ai vue elle-même dans une nouvelle lumière, comme si le mur que je longe depuis mon arrivée ici, par instants un peu moins opaque, soudainement s'amincissait' (p. 245).[VIII] In the travel film about Crete, which he sees twice on successive nights, the pure light of the Mediterranean symbolizes the ideal that he contrasts with the smoke and fog of Bleston, and the first long, lyrical evocation of the sunlit Cretan landscape (pp. 101–02) is echoed at several subsequent points.[11]

But Glissant — conversely and with greater originality — places a key positive value on *opacity* as opposed to transparence; so much so, that in *Le Discours antillais* he says: 'Il faut combattre partout la transparence' (p. 356).[IX] Opacity has a range of overlapping meanings. It can simply signify the recognition of an essentially chaotic reality, an acceptance of the unknown.[12] But it is also an intersubjective concept: the opacity of the Other's difference, which, he argues, the West with its tradition of a universal human essence is unable to accept. Like Butor in *L'Emploi du temps*, but reversing the values given to the terms, Glissant associates light and transparence with the Mediterranean, claiming that the universalist Mediterranean myths imply that 'quelle que soit l'opacité de l'autre pour soi [...], la question sera toujours de ramener cet autre à la transparence vécue par soi: ou bien on l'assimile ou bien on l'annihile' (*Poétique de la Relation*, pp. 61–62).[13] [X]

Clarity, historically, has also been the prerogative of the colonial power: 'La seule clarté enfin, qui fut celle de la présence transcendante de l'autre, de son évidence — colon ou administrateur — d'où nous est né peut-être un tendre goût de l'obscur, et pour moi comme une nécessité, qui est de provoquer l'opaque, le non-évident, de revendiquer

VI 'that wall of clouded glass that separated me from the town of Bleston' (Michel Butor, *Passing Time & A Change of Heart*, translated by Jean Stewart, Simon & Schuster, 1969, p. 51)

VII 'that moment when reality is transformed and purified by the sole power of his keen and accurate vision' (ibid., p. 153)

VIII 'I saw the town itself in a new light, as though the wall alongside which I have been groping ever since my arrival, here and there less opaque, had suddenly grown thinner' (ibid., p. 255)

IX 'We must oppose transparency on all fronts'

X 'no matter how opaque the other is for oneself [...], it will always be a question of reducing this other to the transparency experienced by oneself. Either the other is assimilated, or else it is annihilated.' (Glissant, *Poetics of Relation*, translated by Betsy Wing, University of Michigan, 1997, p. 49) pour chaque collectivité le droit à l'opacité mutuellement consentie' ('Poétique et inconscient martiniquais', p. 237).[XI] Opacity is a *defence* against the objectifying gaze of the other — of, for instance, 'ceux qui nous arrivent d'ailleurs et qui nous partagent illico en rangs qu'ils évaluent', as they are called in *La Case du commandeur* (p. 29).[14] [XII]

XI 'The only clarity, finally, was that of the transcendental presence of the other, of its obviousness – coloniser or administrator – from which perhaps derives our fondness for the obscure, and to me a necessity, that of provoking opacity, the non-evident, of claiming for each community the right to a mutually consented opacity"

XII 'those who come to us from abroad and divide us straight away into ranks to be evaluated"

Opacity, in other words, resists and contests *understanding.* It asserts that the act of understanding, however well-meant, is either an objectifying reduction of the other to pseudo-universal categories, or a false identification of the other with oneself that annuls his difference, or, less often (this is how Glissant defines exoticism), an impossible and dishonest attempt to *become* the other. It is thus always an act of aggression and appropriation.[15] He uses the etymology of the verb 'comprendre' to make this point, seeing in it 'le mouvement des mains qui prennent l'entour et le ramènent à soi. Geste d'enfermement sinon d'appropriation' (*Poétique de la Relation*, p. 206)[XIII]; and contrasting it with a relation that respects the opacity of the other: 'Il ne m'est pas nécessaire que je le "comprenne" pour me sentir solidaire avec lui, pour bâtir avec lui, pour aimer ce qu'il fait. Il ne m'est pas nécessaire de tenter de devenir l'autre (de devenir autre) ni de le "faire" à mon image' (ibid., p. 207).[XIV] This relation is exemplified in a scene in *Le Quatrième* Siècle, between the transported African Longoué and the plantation owner from whom he escaped on his first night as a slave. Many years later they meet in the forest and have a conversation, not in creole but in their 'own' languages — even though Longoué has not used his African language for ten years — so that neither can understand what the other is saying. From this encounter emerges a mutual respect and even complicity:

XIII 'In this version of understanding the verb *to grasp* contains the movement of hands that grab their surroundings and bring them back to themselves. A gesture of enclosure if not appropriation.' (*Poetics of Relation*, trans. B. Wing, p. 190–191)

XIV 'To feel in solidarity with him or to build with him or to like what he does, it is not necessary for me to grasp him. It is not necessary to try to become the other (to become other) nor to "make" him in my image' (ibid., p. 193)

> ils s'accommodèrent du dialogue qui n'en était pas un: l'un et l'autre renfermés chacun sur son propre dommage, et mutuellement inabordables, comme s'ils voilaient d'instinct l'impudeur de la confiance ou comme si, obligés qu'ils étaient de se confier, ils essayaient pourtant de préserver leur libre arbitre ou, plus humainement, leur quant-à-soi. (p. 106)[XV]

XV 'They settled for a dialogue that wasn't one: one and the other, each entrenched in their own suffering, mutually inaccessible, as if they instinctively veiled the immodesty of trust, or as if, compelled as they were to confide in one another, they nonetheless tried to preserve their free will or, in a more human sense, their intimate space.'

More precisely, it is the assumption that one has a *right* to understand that is challenged by the notion of opacity, and the type of understanding that consists in the analysis of objects by detached sovereign observers - whether these are the 'Découvreurs', as he calls the colonizing nations ('vous, voyageurs aussi, qui pensez le monde sans vous mêler à lui' (*L'Intention poétique*, p. 16))[16] [XVI] or later ethnographers.[17]

Objective analysis can never be adequate: the chaotic complexities of the world are such that 'Le *regard constitutif* ni l'analyse ne suffisent à les débrouiller: si tu n'es pas drame et mêlée en ce chaos, tu tariras dans ta clarté ôtée' (ibid., p. 24).[XVII] The kind of participatory understanding that he is recommending is intersubjective, and accepts its own limitations; also, it often works indirectly and intuitively. In *Le Discours antillais* he describes the visit of a Haitian theatre group to Fort-de-France; because of the differences between Haitian and Martinican creole, the audience could not understand very much of the dialogue, but, he says, 'cette opacité même nous confirmait dans l'idée que c'était là *notre* théâtre. Il y a des manières inédites de comprendre ...' (p. 265).[XVIII]

XVI 'you, travelers also, who consider the world without mixing with it' (Éduoard Glissant, *Poetic Intention*, trans. Nathalie Stephens with Anne Malena, Nightboat Books, 2010, p. 12)

XVII 'Neither the constitutive gaze nor analysis are enough to disentangle them: if you are not drama and melee in this chaos, you will dry out in your removed clarity.' (ibid., p. 20)

XVIII 'this very opaqueness made us feel that this was our theater. There are unknown ways of understanding ...' (*Caribbean Discourse*, trans. J.M. Dash, p. 155)

A frequent image for opacity is the forest covering the mountainous north of Martinique, where the maroons — the escaped slaves — lived: 'La forêt du marronnage fut ainsi le premier obstacle que l'esclave en fuite opposait à la *transparence* du colon. Il n'y a pas de chemin évident, pas de *ligne*, dans ce touffu. On y tourne sans transparence, jusqu'à la souche première' (*Le Discours antillais*, p. 150).[XIX] Its density and darkness provide a 'refuge miséricordieux' (*Mahagony*, p. 90)[XX]; the forest becomes emblematic of the island as a whole — 'Et la parole de mon paysage est d'abord forêt, qui sans arrêt foisonne' (*Le Discours antillais*, p. 255).[XXI] This offers an exact contrast to the negative connotations of the forest in Butor's *La Modification*, in which Léon, looking at the forest of Fontainebleau through the train window, imagines a *mise en scène* of his own situation as 'un homme en difficulté qui voudrait se sauver [...] comme s'il était perdu dans [...] une forêt se refermant en quelque sorte derrière lui sans qu'il arrive même à retrouver quel est le chemin qui l'a conduit là, car les branches et les lianes masquent les traces de son passage' (pp. 198–99).[XXII]

XIX 'The forest of the maroon was thus the first obstacle the slave opposed to the *transparency* of the planter. There is no clear path, no way *forward*, in this density. You turn in obscure circles until you find the primordial tree.' (ibid., p. 83)

XX 'merciful refuge'

XXI 'the language of my landscape is primarily that of the forest, which unceasingly bursts with life' (ibid., p. 146)

XXII 'a man in difficulties who wants to save himself [...] as if he were lost in [...] a forest that somehow closes up behind him so that he cannot even recognize the path that brought him there, for branches and the lianas have covered his tracks' (*Passing Time & A Change of Heart*, trans. J. Stewart, p. 481)

If, then, Butor and Glissant attach opposite values to the concepts of transparence and opacity, what is the relationship between this opposition and their respective conceptions of *history*? These are also very different, and in ways that reflect their own positions within it. Glissant is concerned with the history of the Caribbean, much of which remains unknown. For him, therefore, history can never be transparent; the psychological and cultural need to recover as much of it as possible has to be balanced against an acceptance of its 'opacity' — a realization that its unknowability does not diminish its importance for the present. The fragments that are known do not add up to a full, linear account; and if knowledge of the period of slavery is chaotic and fragmented (the 'maelstrom', as it is called in

Mahagony), there is an even more irremediable opacity attaching to the earlier history of the Caribbean slaves: the fact of transportation from Africa, which obliterates their previous existence and marks their history with an absolute cut-off point. 'Les Antilles sont le lieu d'une histoire faite de ruptures et dont le commencement est un arrachement brutal, la Traite' (*Le Discours antillais*, p. 130).[XXIII] This, Glissant argues, means that history for the Martinicans is not simply a finite gap in their knowledge, but a conceptual impossibility:

XXIII 'The French Caribbean is the site of a history characterized by ruptures and that began with a brutal dislocation, the slave trade.' (*Caribbean Discourse*, trans. J.M. Dash, p. 61)

> Notre conscience historique ne pouvait pas 'sédimenter', si on peut ainsi dire, de manière progressive et continue, comme chez les peuples qui ont engendré une philosophie souvent totalitaire de l'histoire, les peuples européens, mais s'agrégeait sous les auspices du choc, de la contraction, de la négation douloureuse et de l'explosion. Ce discontinu dans le continu, et l'impossibilité pour la conscience collective d'en faire le tour, caractérisent ce que j'appelle une non-histoire. (ibid., pp. 130–31)[XXIV]

XXIV 'Our historical consciousness could not be deposited gradually and continuously like sediment, as it were, as happened with those peoples who have frequently produced a totalitarian philosophy of history, for instance European peoples, but came together in the context of shock, contraction, painful negation, and explosive forces. This dislocation of the continuum, and the inability of the collective consciousness to absorb it all, characterize what I call a non-history.' (ibid., p. 62)

For the Africans, therefore, their arrival in the Caribbean was a completely and violently new beginning. Papa Longoué claims that history *starts* with the arrival of his ancestor, the first Longoué: 'Ce serait le premier jour le deuxième si tu veux, et non pas comment déjà un matin de juillet 1788, car qui connaît juillet et qui connaît 1788 pour lui pour moi c'est le premier jour le premier cri le soleil et la première lune et le premier siècle du pays' (p. 74).[XXV] This was not at all the case for the European settlers: Glissant comments that 'les maîtres et les chiens [...] n'entraient pas dans cette autre histoire', because for them it was simply a continuation of their old life — 'bientôt ils voudraient continuer par ici leur terre' (*L'Intention poétique*, p. 7).[XXVI] This echoes very closely Butor's view of the European settlers in America, who in *Mobile* are shown as reproducing in America the Europe that they had nevertheless rejected: 'ne fallait-il point reconstituer autour de soi une nouvelle Europe, effacer le plus possible de son esprit ce continent qui nous accueillait mais nous effrayait?' (p. 99).[XXVII]

XXV 'It would be the first day the second if you will, and not like a morning of July 1788, for who knows July and who knows 1788, for me for you it is the first day, the first cry, the sun, the first moon, and the first century of the country.'

XXVI 'But they were not entering into this other history: masters and dogs had come for plunder and profit, soon they would want to extend their land into these parts' (*Poetic Intention*, trans. N. Stephens et al., p.3)

XXVII 'should we not endeavour to rebuild a new Europe around us, erasing as much as possible from our mind that continent that welcomed us but also frightened us?'

The difference between Caribbean and European history, then, can be characterized in terms of continuity and discontinuity. Thus Butor's representations of history always presuppose that it is fully recoverable. The ideal of transparence suggests the possibility of looking back *through* the intervening 'layers' of time to a primordial past: thus the 'azure' of present-day Crete '*renvoyait* surtout à un moment beaucoup plus ancien et plus étalé [...] cet azur qui nous renvoyait à l'époque où ces monuments étaient villes et non vestiges, à l'intérieur du bleu du ciel qui proclamait sa *permanence*, sa *continuité* avec celui qui s'étendait, pur, bénéfique, immense, sur la jeunesse de ces palais et de ces temples (p. 228, my emphasis).[XXVIII] Through the various travel documentaries that Jacques sees at the cinema, he can establish a continuity going back from Rome, through Athens and Crete to the ancient archaeological sites of Petra, Baalbeck and Timgad (p. 241, and 243); and Bleston itself is traced back to its origin as the Roman town Belli Civitas, whose layout can be seen 'through' the buildings of the present city: 'Bleston, Bellista, Belli Civitas, au deuxième siècle après Jésus-Christ, quadrilatère fortifié au milieu des forêts et marais, avec ses petits thermes, avec son temple de la guerre à l'emplacement même [...] du chœur de l'Ancienne Cathédrale, et la croix centrale de son quadrillage de rues dallées à l'emplacement même de l'angle sud-ouest de la place de l'Hôtel de Ville' (p. 244).[XXIX]

XXVIII 'that blue which [...], above all, sent one back to a far more distant, more extensive past [...] that blue which sent us back to the period when these monuments were cities and not ruins, the blue of that sky which proclaimed its permanence, its continuity with the sky that spread, pure, beneficent and immense, when these palaces and these temples were new.' (*Passing Time & A Change of Heart*, trans. J. Stewart, p. 238)

XXIX 'Bleston, Bellista, Belli Civitas, in the second century A.P., a fortified square surrounded by forests and marshes, with its little thermae, its temple of war on the very site [...] of the choir of the Old Cathedral, and the central cross of its grid of paved streets on the very site of the southeastern corner of Town Hall Square' (ibid., p. 254)

Jacques's main project is the recovery of his own personal past — the year in Bleston — and the method for achieving this relies on the *unbroken* stretch of time involved; he works his way back gradually through the accumulated intervening layers to a solid original foundation, 'le sol d'antan' (p. 120),[XXX] 'mesurant alors l'épaisseur de cette matière qu'il faut que je sonde et tamise, afin de retrouver des assises et des fondations' (ibid.).[XXXI] This quasi-archaeological excavation of the past is possible only because all the intermediate layers form a continuous, supporting sequence — an 'immense échafaudage de poutres vivantes' with 'à des niveaux intermédiaires toute une série de *relais* ou d'*échelons* sur lesquels mon effort de mémoire ce soir *prenait appui* pour parvenir jusqu'à ce sol d'antan' (p. 289, my emphasis).[XXXII] But his personal experience of present-day Bleston has all along been guided by representations of past cultures (for instance, the eighteenth-century French tapestries in its museum which portray the life of Theseus) and it is thus not surprising that right at the end of the novel the 'archaeological' method of recapturing the past is suddenly seen to extend back far beyond his own memories:

XXX 'the original soil' (ibid., 125)

XXXI 'gaug[ing] the thickness of the silt which I must plumb and filter in order to recover my bedrock, my foundations.' (ibid.)

XXXII 'a huge scaffolding of living branches' with 'at different levels a whole series of footholds by means of which, this evening, my straining memory has climbed down to reach that ground of long ago.' (ibid., p. 299)

> chaque monument, chaque objet, chaque image nous renvoyant à d'autres périodes [...], d'autres périodes souvent lointaines et oubliées dont l'épaisseur et la distance se mesurent non plus par semaines ou par mois mais par siècles, [...] comme celles, qui se superposaient dans ma vision samedi, tandis que je regardais les tapisseries du Musée [...] ces points noués en France au dix-

huitième siècle, par lesquels m'atteignaient [*sic*] [...] une légende très antique transmise par la culture latine, par ce grec impérial Plutarque [...], une légende dont l'ordonnance datait de la puissance d'Athènes, et à travers laquelle toute une histoire antérieure se transmettait, perpétuant le nom de Minos, rappelant un arrangement de la réalité très fondamental et très recouvert. (pp. 294–95)[XXXIII]

XXXIII 'every monument, every object, every image sending us back to other periods [...], other periods often remote and forgotten, whose density and distance are to be measured not by weeks or months but by centuries, [...] like those that came into my mind's eye on Saturday while I was looking at the Museum tapestries [...] those links forged in France in the eighteenth century through which there has come down to me [...] a very ancient legend transmitted through the culture of Rome, by a Greek of the Roman Empire, Plutarch [...], a legend that first took shape in the days of Athens' glory, through which a whole long story of earlier days was handed down, perpetuating the name of Minos and recalling an arrangement of reality which was both fundamental and highly recondite.' (ibid., p. 305)

In other words, there may be gaps in our knowledge of history but with determination and patience these can be filled in. The notion of a distant historical past is extremely powerful in Butor's writing precisely because it is the deeply buried but recoverable *foundation* of the present.

Thus for Butor, the issue is the re-connection, in the present, of the individual with the historical forces that have shaped his or her life. It is the repression of these links that has to be overcome; the problem is for the individual — Léon Delmont in *La Modification*, for instance — to become conscious of exactly how the historical determinations have worked out in his particular case. He has to understand how the 'myth' of imperial Rome has affected his own life: 'essayant de le faire tourner sous votre regard à l'intérieur de l'espace historique, afin d'améliorer votre connaissance des liaisons qu'il a avec les conduites et décisions de vous-même et de ceux qui vous entourent' (p. 238).[XXXIV] But the assumption is always that history itself is solid, knowable and continuous, and goes back for ever.

XXXIV 'trying to see around it in the light of history, so as to know more about its connections with the behavior and the decisions of those around you' (ibid., p. 518)

For both authors, therefore, history involves a sense of loss, but the loss is located differently. In the case of Butor's heroes, it is a feeling of separation from the plenitude of the past. Delmont, for instance, eventually realizes that his confusions and frustrations are due to an unconscious yearning for the time 'où le monde avait un centre' (p. 277)[XXXV] — in other words, a nostalgia for empire. Once he has made this connection, he can come to terms with the fact that 'Si puissant pendant tant de siècles sur tous les rêves européens, le souvenir de l'Empire est maintenant une figure insuffisante pour désigner l'avenir de ce monde, devenu pour chacun de nous beaucoup plus vaste et tout autrement distribué' (ibid.).[XXXVI] That is, he can fill in the gaps between the Roman empire and the present, and thus re-establish himself more authentically and more securely in 'his' history. The sense of loss, in other words, derives from a gap *between* the historical past and the present; and the ideal is for the individual to become aware of himself as grounded in history as a point of origin. The existence of the 'sol d'antan' is never in doubt.

XXXV 'in which the world had a center' (ibid., p. 555)

XXXVI 'The memory of the Empire, which dominated all the dreams of Europe for so many centuries, is now no longer an adequate image to represent the future of the world, which for each one of us has become far vaster and quite differently organized.' (ibid.)

Whereas for Glissant, the loss is of history itself. Such historical knowledge as has been recovered is eroded by the massive, engulfing absence of the pre-transportation period, which *La Case du commandeur* calls 'le trou du temps'.[XXXVII] In this situation, there is no point of origin to look back to. Moreover, transportation is such a total change that it destroys the *identity* of those who undergo it: Longoué on his arrival in Martinique is 'Cet homme qui n'avait plus de souche, ayant roulé dans l'unique vague déferlante du voyage [...] et qui n'était pas encore Longoué' (p. 83).[XXXVIII] The chapter of *Le Discours antillais* which addresses this topic starts by stating: 'Il y a différence entre le déplacement [...] d'un peuple qui se continue ailleurs et le transbord (la traite) d'une population qui ailleurs *se change en autre chose*' (p. 28).[XXXIX] The difference is that the former 'maintient l'Etre' (p. 29) while the latter do not ('Nous renonçons à l'Etre' (p. 28)).[XL] In other words, transportation makes it impossible to preserve an idealist conception of individual identity as permanent Being: as he expresses it earlier, in *L'Intention poétique*: 'Nous ne naquîmes pas, nous fûmes déportés d'Est en Ouest. Un couteau de marin trancha le cordon ombilical. Des fers d'esclave arrêtèrent le sang. Il n'y a là nulle essence, mais perdition' (p. 197).[XLI]

And yet this 'perdition' proves to be the starting point for a new and positive realization. The loss of origin and of an essentialist identity opens up a way into what Glissant calls 'la Relation'; thus, returning to the text in *Le Discours antillais*, the transported people who 'renounce being' 'entre ainsi dans la variance toujours recommencée de la Relation (du relais, du relatif)' (p. 29).[XLII] And he goes on to explain:

> Il n'y a pas là seulement agonie et perdition mais l'occasion aussi d'affirmer un ensemble estimable de propriétés. Celle par exemple de fréquenter les 'valeurs' non plus comme absolu de référence mais comme modes agissants d'une Relation (Le renoncement aux pures valeurs d'origine ouvre sur un sens inédit de la mise en rapports.) Celle aussi de critiquer plus naturellement une conception de l'universel transparent..... (pp. 29–30)[XLIII]

'La Relation' — a central concept in Glissant's theoretical work — is a non-hierarchical, non-reductive relation to the Other. To the notions of essence and universality, it opposes a recognition of otherness in its particularity and diversity: 'Le Même requiert l'Etre, le Divers établit la Relation' (*Le Discours antillais*, p. 190).[XLIV] Also, the permanence and

XXXVII 'the hole of time'

XXXVIII 'this man who no longer had roots, having rolled in the single crashing wave of travel [...] and who had not yet become Longoué'

XXXIX 'There is a difference between the transplanting [...] of a people who continue to survive elsewhere and the transfer (by the slave trade) of a population to another place where they change into something different' (*Caribbean Discourse*, trans. J.M. Dash, p. 14)

XL The difference is the former '*maintains its original nature*' while the latter do not ('We abandon the idea of fixed being') (ibid., p. 14–15)

XLI 'We were not born, we were deported, from East to West. A sailor's knife cut the umbilical cord. Slave irons stopped the blood. There is no essence there, but perdition' (*Poetic Intention*, trans N. Stephens et al., p. 183.)

XLII 'thus enters the constantly shifting and variable process of creolization (of relationship, of relativity)' (*Caribbean Discourse*, trans. J.M. Dash, p. 15)

XLIII 'Therein lie not only distress and loss but also the opportunity to assert a considerable set of possibilities. For instance, the possibility of dealing with "values" no longer in absolute terms but as active agents of synthesis. (The abandonment of pure original values allows for an unprecedented potential for contact.) Also the possibility of criticizing more naturally a conception of universal anonymity...' (ibid., p. 16)

XLIV 'Sameness requires fixed Being, Diversity establishes Becoming' (ibid., p. 98)

XLV 'the modern tendency among cultures, in their wanderings, their "structural" need for an unreserved equality' (ibid., p. 98)

singularity of *origin* is replaced by *'métissage'* — mixed, changing cultures constituted within a network of fluid 'relations': 'l'implication moderne des cultures, dans leurs errances, leur revendication "structurelle" d'une égalité sans réserve' (ibid., p. 191).[XLV] Relation thus rejoins the notion of opacity — it is 'l'implication d'opacités sauves et intégrées' (*L'Intention poétique*, p. 41) — as an engagement with the density of the Other: 'la poétique de la relation suppose qu'à chacun soit proposée la densité (l'opacité) de l'autre. Plus l'autre résiste dans son épaisseur ou sa fluidité [...] plus sa réalité devient expressive, et plus la relation féconde' (ibid., p. 23).[XLVI]

XLVI 'Relation thus rejoins the notion of opacity – it is "the implication of spared and integrated opacities" (*Poetic Intention*, p. 34) – as an engagement with the density of the Other: 'the poetics of relation assumes that to each is proposed the density (the opacity) of the other. The more the other resists in his thickness or his fluidity (without being limited to it), the more his reality becomes expressive, and the more fecund the relation' (ibid., p. 18)

The absence of historical origin, then, leads to a conception of existence as a plurality of relations with otherness (and both of these are aspects of opacity). 'Relation' is above all an attitude to cultural difference. Thus a particular attitude to history, an attempt to wrest something positive from the trauma and lack underlying Caribbean history, ends up as an ethical framework for conceptualizing cultural difference.

How does Butor fit into this? Does his contrary assumption of a secure historical origin and his privileging of transparence and understanding result in an opposite attitude to cultural difference? In fact, the situation is not as neatly symmetrical as that. An important emphasis throughout his work is the way in which a new understanding of the other rebounds on one's view of oneself: unlike Glissant's ethnographer (see note 17), Butor's observer cannot remain unchanged by the results of his observation, as the very title of volume 3 of *Génie du lieu — Boomerang* — implies. In *Degrés*, also, the teacher Pierre Vernier is at pains to show his class how profoundly the discovery of America altered the picture which Europe had of itself; and he is, further, aware of how differently this information is interpreted by his black pupil Maurice Tangala: 'je vois son visage noir, ses lèvres sombres, sourire tout autrement que les vôtres' (p. 91).[18][XLVII]

XLVII 'I see his black face, his dark lips smile quite differently from yours' (Michel Butor, *Degrees. A Novel*, translated by Richard Howard, Simon & Schuster, 1961, p. 80)

But this could simply be a consequence of Butor's structuralism; it is the nature of structures that a change in one element has repercussions on all the others. And structures exist to achieve transparence: 'un moyen de forcer le réel à se révéler' (*Essais sur le roman*, p. 17).[19][XLVIII] The arduous quest for intellectual transparence is very prominent in Butor's earlier work. Jacques Revel, as we have seen, struggles to reduce the alien environment of Bleston to transparent signification. Moreover, this is an openly aggressive operation — the town 'se refuse à l'examen comme si la lumière la brûlait, telle une femme dont on ne pourrait apercevoir le visage qu'en arrachant son voile avec violence' (p. 105) [XLIX] — which works through a purifying but corrosive fire:

XLVIII 'a means to force reality to reveal itself'

XLIX '[the town] shuns scrutiny as though the light scorched it, like a woman whose face one cannot see except by forcibly tearing away her veil' (*Passing Time & A Change of Heart*, p. 108)

'Bleston dont je ronge la carapace par cette écriture, par cette lente flamme acharnée' (p. 296) which aims to '[transformer] leur sable en verre' (p. 297).[L]

In a discussion of *L'Emploi du temps* with Georges Charbonnier,[20] Butor makes it clear that understanding is the prime value and the only basis for the hero's survival: 'Est-ce que le personnage va être capable de comprendre ce qui se passe autour de lui ou non. S'il est capable de comprendre, ça va, il est sauvé et il pourra sortir; s'il n'est pas capable de comprendre il sera écrasé' (*Entretiens...*, p. 95).[LI] Given Jacques's vulnerable and disorientated state, it is slightly surprising that he always assumes he understands the feelings of Bleston's inhabitants, attributing to them en masse for instance 'une tranquillité précaire, péniblement acquise à grand acharnement, à grande résistance et patience, à grande usure, à grands renoncements, enfoncements et abandons, à grands ensevelissements, obscurcissements et trahisons, à grandes humiliations bues, exigences tues, à grands secrets perdus, à grands oublis' (pp. 122–23).[LII] He also rather patronizingly assumes that they are unable to understand him, and that they see him as a fabulous exotic creature from a more enlightened world; James Jenkins's dream of visiting the continent 'nous fait encore, Lucien et moi, tant briller de prestige à ses yeux, comme ambassadeurs de l'outre-mer' (p. 91);[LIII] and his landlady 'me considère toujours comme un être d'une espèce particulière, [...] dont il ne faut pas chercher à comprendre les habitudes, bizarrement élevé, bizarrement ignorant de choses qu'elle considère elle-même comme tellement évidentes, [...] mais en communication effective avec cette région de la réalité, pour elle quasi fabuleuse, le continent' (p. 109).[LIV]

Jacques is also guilty of a kind of appropriation of Horace Buck, the African immigrant he becomes friends with in Bleston and whom he sees as 'l'incarnation de mon propre malheur' (p. 95).[LV] His desire to wreak revenge on Bleston by *burning* it is acted out by Horace: while his own minor and symbolic act of burning the map of the town fills him with shame; he rejoices in the numerous real arson attacks which he attributes to Horace: 'je sentais la flamme courir, gagner la ville; je la sentais, avec une intense satisfaction vengeresse' (p. 226).[LVI] Horace represents, for Jacques, the 'darker' side of his consciousness, and at the same time conforms to the stereotype of the mindlessly violent black man. Jacques's criticism of his landlady's racist horror of black men as violent animals (p. 108) is thus undermined by his own, less conscious, association of Horace with blind aggression.

L 'I can wear down your carapace, Bleston, that slow relentless flame issuing from your own innards' which aims to '[transform] their sand to glass' (ibid., p. 307)

LI 'Is the character able to understand what's happening around him or not? If he can understand, then fine, he's saved and will escape; if he can't understand, he will be crushed'

LII 'a precarious peace awaited them, peace painfully acquired at the cost of relentless efforts, great stubbornness and patience, long attrition, with so much renounced and rejected, so much buried, besmirched and betrayed, so many humiliations endured, so many needs unfulfilled, so many vital secrets lost, so much forgotten' (ibid., p. 127)

LIII 'which, to this day, confers such glamour on Lucien and myself, ambassadors from a land beyond the sea' (ibid., p. 93)

LIV 'She still considers me as a being of a peculiar species, [...] whose habits are incomprehensible, a being oddly brought up, oddly ignorant of things that she herself considers self-evident, [...] and who nevertheless is actually in contact with that almost fabulous region, the Continent.' (ibid., p. 112)

LV 'the embodiment of my own misfortune' (ibid., p. 97)

LVI 'I felt the conflagration growing, spreading over the town; I felt it with intense vindictive satisfaction' (ibid., p. 236)

Mobile, published six years later, is subtitled 'Étude pour une représentation des États-Unis', and consists mainly of a collage of quotations from a wide range of American texts. The contrast with *L'Emploi du temps* is clear: rather than a single narrative viewpoint which filters and 'understands' its alien surroundings, the intertextual approach adopted in *Mobile* preserves the full opacity and diversity of America's texts.[21] The authorial voice is almost non-existent; there is little in the way of explanation, and so one's overall impression is indeed of the *resistance* of this reality to the European's (author's or reader's) attempt to understand it.

It is, however, noticeable that one major community is not given its own voice: the Afro-Americans. These figure in the text only as the *object* of other people's, mainly racist, discourse (in particular, Jefferson's *Notes on the State of Virginia*). They are thus presented sympathetically, as victims of white oppression. However, since the basic principle of *Mobile* is to juxtapose elements of American culture in as 'raw' a form as possible, it must be significant that the black community has no unmediated documentary presence in the text but appears only through the discourses which talk *about* it. A major example is Butor's fictional recreation of the voice of the white South expressing its feelings towards black people, which does at one point, towards the end, include that of a man who has a secret romantic involvement with a woman (pp. 287–92, intermittently) and who we eventually realize is black when he says:

LVII 'Don't be afraid, / nothing much will happen to you, / I'll share a bit of my darkness, / there'll be some sand left in your hair'

> n'aie pas peur,
> il ne t'arrivera presque rien,
> je vais te passer un peu de ma noirceur,
> il restera un peu de sable dans tes cheveux (p. 291)[LVII]

— but this still contrasts markedly with the 'authentic', documentary extracts from texts of other communities. One can, perhaps, interpret the absence of black American voices in *Mobile* as a deliberate signaling of Butor's own awareness of the limitations of his perspective and hence of his own cultural specificity — of himself, that is, *as* a European. As such, he is perhaps, for some reason, simply unable to represent Afro-Americans as subjects. Moreover, this could be a form of opacity: in an article on William Faulkner called 'Sur l'opacité', Glissant notes how Faulkner describes his black characters are solely represented from the outside, never revealing their thoughts and feelings — and this, he claims, is in itself a kind of respect for the opacity of the other: 'Ils opposent ainsi à Faulkner lui-même un non *au-delà* qu'il ne franchira jamais. Autrement dit: l'incapacité de Faulkner à cerner ce personnage est *positive*. Elle signale que l'entreprise de l'auteur est intègre et absolue à tous les étages; et aussi que le Noir américain oppose une réelle densité (ce qui en Amérique était jusqu'ici à affirmer)' (*L'Intention poétique*, p. 177).[LVIII] Thus, something missing from the representation can be a sign of honesty and respect rather than a blind spot.

LVIII 'They thus oppose to Faulkner himself a *not-beyond* into which he will never cross. In other words: Faulkner's inability to apprehend this character is *positive*. It signals that the author's enterprise is integral and absolute at all stages; and also that the American Black opposes a real density (that which was yet in America to be affirmed).' (*Poetic Intention*, trans. N. Stephens et al., p. 163)

But one still needs to ask why this gap occurs only in the case of Afro-Americans — especially since it contrasts so strikingly with the way in which the American Indians are treated in the text. Here we are given a considerable amount of factual information on Indian history, many individuals are named, and many of their speeches are quoted at length.[22] There is, in other words, an attempt to represent the historical reality of the Indians and, through their own texts, to engage intersubjectively with their otherness. And it is precisely this contrast that provides a clue to the reason for the absence of the black American voice. In the course of a discussion of *Mobile* with Charbonnier, Butor says: 'Le problème indien aux États-Unis est beaucoup plus enfoncé, beaucoup plus souterrain que le problème noir. Le problème "Noir", ça tout le monde en parle. Et on sait que les Noirs ne disparaîtront pas. Tandis que pour les Indiens...' (*Entretiens…*, p. 229).[LIX] In other words, the Indians are a more important 'problem' than the black community — and this priority turns out to be based on the Indians' status as the *indigenous* people of America. Butor has just argued that American society is *founded* upon the guilt of the expropriation and murder of the Indians (ibid., p. 228); and elsewhere, in an article on Faulkner, he states that 'La faute originelle du Sud, ce n'est pas l'esclavage; celui-ci n'est que l'inéluctable conséquence de l'appropriation indue de la terre' (*Essais sur les modernes*, p. 353).[23] [LX] It is as though the temporal and logical priority of the aggression towards the Indians affects its moral evaluation: the oppression of the Indians is more serious than that of the slaves because the Indians are the *original* inhabitants of the continent.

LIX 'The Indian problem in the United States is far more entrenched, far more insidious than the Black problem. The 'Black' problem everyone talks about. And we know Black people won't disappear. Whereas with Indian people...'

LX 'Slavery wasn't the original sin of the South; it is merely the inevitable consequence of the wrongful appropriation of the land'

Mobile itself claims that the importation of African slaves was motivated by the settlers' relation to the Indians: not only could the Indians not be made to work on the plantations, but the settlers were afraid of them, and there was therefore a psychological need to import an inferior people that they could dominate:

> Et l'Indien, expression, visage, langage de ce continent scandaleux, inspirait trop de terreur pour qu'on pût le faire travailler […] aussi, comme on […] voulait renverser cette inégalité qui vous avait chassés de votre pays, afin d'avoir auprès de soi un plus pauvre que soi vous enrichissant, plutôt que de tenter de domestiquer l'Indien, on préféra importer de faux indigènes… (p. 107)[LXI]

LXI 'And the Indian, the expression, face and language of this outrageous continent, inspired too much terror for him to be put to work […] so, as they [….] wanted to overturn this inequality that had driven you out of your country, in order to have someone poorer than yourself by your side enriching you, rather than attempting to domesticate the Indian, they preferred to import false natives…'

While the text obviously does not support this action or the mentality attributed to it, it does seem to concur in the privileged status implicitly accorded to the *indigenous* people of America. The Indian, as the original inhabitant, is the true 'expression, visage, langage' of the continent, and the Africans are merely a 'false' substitute.

It is as though Butor's European perspective can understand and represent an otherness that is a pure indigenous origin, but not one that derives from 'la Traite'. Thus *Mobile*'s refusal to include black Americans on the same terms as Indians in its intertextual 'polyphony' of American voices can ultimately be explained in terms of the importance, which, as we have already seen, Butor attaches to the notion of historical origin. In their very different ways, Glissant and Butor both show how one's relation to the cultural other is ultimately driven by one's conception of history.

University of Aberdeen
Celia Britton

1 *La Modification* (Éditions de Minuit, 1957). Place of publication of all books cited is Paris unless otherwise stated.

2 *Le Quatrième Siècle* (Éditions du Seuil, 1964).

3 *Le Génie du lieu* (Grasset, 1958). Two subsequent volumes have been published with Gallimard: *Où* (1972) and *Boomerang* (1978).

4 *L'Emploi du temps* (Éditions de Minuit, 1956).

5 *Degrés* (Gallimard, 1960).

6 *Mobile* (Gallimard, 1962).

7 'Poétique et inconscient martiniquais', in *Identité culturelle et francophonie dans les Amériques*, ed. by E. Snyder and A. Valdman (Quebec, Presses de l'Université de Laval, 1976).

8 *Mahagony* (Éditions du Seuil, 1987).

9 *Le Discours antillais* (Éditions du Seuil, 1981).

10 He says to Georges Charbonnier: 'Je me suis senti plus à l'étranger dans le nord de l'Angleterre que dans la vallée du Nil, j'étais plus loin de chez moi, j'avais plus de difficulté à me retrouver moi-même en Angleterre qu'en Égypte, et cela m'a fait beaucoup réfléchir parce que je ne m'y attendais pas' (*Entretiens avec Michel Butor* (Gallimard, 1967), p. 98). ['I felt more like a foreigner in the North of England than in the Nile Valley, I felt further from home and had a harder time finding myself in England than in Egypt, and this gave me a lot to think about because I would have never expected it']

11 For instance: in Bleston, even in summer, the skies are only 'presque bleus' ['almost blue'] and 'on est loin encore de cet azur qui règne sur les esplanades [...] de la Crète' (p. 115) ['how different, still, from that azure which reigns above the esplanades [...] of the ruined palaces of Crete'] (*Passing Time & A Change of Heart*, trans. Jean Stewart (London, Simon & Schuster, 1969). Also, it does not last long; the approach of autumn will bring fog and 'blindness': 'L'ennemi [...] les contaminera de plus en plus profondément de brumes; de plus en plus de taies recouvriront l'œil de leurs caux' (p. 115) ['The enemy will [...] will taint them ever more deeply with its fogs; an ever thicker film will veil that faraway blue which, so briefly, had drawn nearer.' (ibid., p. 119)].

12 The novel *Malemort* (Éditions du Seuil, 1975) castigates those who prefer 'cette clarté sotte douce à l'empan de minuit qu'il eût fallu accepter de traverser pour se connaître vraiment' (p. 166) [this silly clarity, sweet at the stroke of midnight, which one would have had to accept to cross in order to truly know oneself], and who attack the narrator for his 'obscurity'; 'Tous criant: "Mais qu'est-ce que ça veut dire? Soyez clair, parlez clair et net, parlez pour nous", dans ce balan de tourments dont pas un ne saurait clarifier le fond ni arrêter le mouvement' (p. 190) [All of them shouting: 'But what do you mean? Be clear, speak clearly and plainly, speak for us', in this tumult of torments of which none could clarify the meaning or stop the movement].

13 *Poétique de la Relation* (Editions du Seuil, 1990).

14 *La Case du commandant* (Éditions du Seuil, 1981).

15 In *Le Discours antillais* he refers to three accounts by Europeans of Martinican society: Lafcadio Hearn in 1865, Maud Mannoni's analysis of a Martinican psychiatric patient in France, and Jack Corsani's literary history of the French Caribbean, and comments: 'Il s'agit là de trois regards portés par une sympathie évidente. Notre hypothèse de travail est que cette sympathie originelle diffuse malgré elle une agression réelle contre le Martiniquais [...] le regard de l'autre vise à abolir le Martiniquais, soit qu'il le rature par exotisation, ou l'élide par transparence, ou le chosifie dans une minutie totalisante' (p. 304) [There we have three different viewpoints shaped by an evident sense of sympathy. Our working hypothesis is that this original sympathy, in spite of its intentions, generates a real aggression against the Martinican [...] the gaze of the other seeks to abolish the Martinican, whether erasing him through exoticization, eliding him in the name of transparency, or objectifying him in totalising minutiae.]

16 *L'Intention poétique* (Éditions du Seuil, 1969).

17 The typical ethnographer reduces his subjects to objects of his observation: La méfiance que nous lui vouons ne provient pas du déplaisir d'être regardés, mais de l'obscur ressentiment de ne pas voir à notre tour' (*L'Intention poétique*, p. 135) ['The distrust we feel toward it comes not from the displeasure at being watched, but from the resentment at not watching in turn' (*Poetic Intention*, trans. Nathalie Stephens with Anna Malena, New York: Nightboat Books, 2010, p. 122)]. But it is possible for the ethnographer's understanding comes through intersubjective participation in reality, as in the case of Michel Leiris, of whom Glissant writes: '"L'observateur attentif" qu'est (ou était) l'ethnographe devra *s'inscrire au drame du monde*: par-delà son analytique – en principe "solitaire" – il devra vivre une poétique (un partage). Ainsi Leiris' (ibid., p. 135) ['"The attentive observer" that is the ethnographer must *inscribe himself in the drama of the world*: beyond his analysis – in principle, "solitary" – he must live a poetics (sharing). Thus Leiris' (ibid., p. 122)]

18 The intersubjective nature of understanding other cultures is also emphasized in *Genie du lieu I*, where he writes: 'le plus humble paysan égyptien [...] se trouve devant l'obligation de situer l'histoire européenne, l'histoire telle qu'elle est réfléchie par un de ces Européens qu'il peut rencontrer dans les rues de Caire ou dans les hôtels de Louqsor, à l'intérieur d'un contexte beaucoup plus vaste, tâche énorme, tâche monstrueuse, mais si urgente qu'il est certain que commencera bientôt sa réalisation et que s'inventera, se répandra dans ce pays, comme dans tous les grands pays d'Orient en bouleversement, une façon nouvelle de considérer et d'interpréter l'histoire qui réagira forcément sur celle de l'Europe elle-même, apportant d'immenses changements d'accentuation et de perspective' (p. 193). [the humblest Egyptian farmer [...] finds himself obligated to situate European history, history as it is reflected by one of those Europeans he encounters in the streets of Cairo or in the hotels of Louksor, considered within a much wider context, a huge task, a monstruous task, but one so urgent its realisation will surely soon begin, and a new way of considering and interpreting history will be invented and spread throughout this country, as in all the great Eastern countries in upheaval, one that will inevitably react on Europe's own history, bringing immense changes in emphasis and perspective.]

19 *Essais sur le roman* (Gallimard, 1960).

20 Georges Charbonnier: *Entretiens avec Michel Butor* (Gallimard, 1967).

21 Butor explains to Charbonnier why he wanted to get away from the normal 'récit de voyage' in which the author *tells* the reader what the country is like: 'Bien sûr, ce que ces auteurs disaient était exact, les anecdotes qu'ils racontaient on ne pouvait pas les contester, [...] mais ces anecdotes n'étaient pas dans leur lumière véritable, c'est-à-dire qu'on ne pouvait pas, véritablement, en tirer des conséquences sérieuses. Cela n'était pas dans l'espace américain' (*Entretiens...*, 156). [Of course, what those authors were saying was true, one couldn't argue against the anecdotes they'd tell, [...] but these anecdotes weren't in their true light, which is to say that one couldn't, truly, draw serious conclusions from them. This didn't exist in the American space.]

22 e.g. pp. 229–30: 'En 1855, le chef indien Seattle, qui donna son nom à la plus importante cité de Washington, autrefois nommé New York, déclara aux négociateurs européens: "Toutes les parcelles de ce sol sont sacrées" ...', followed by ten lines of text quoting from his speech. [In 1855, the Indian chief Seattle, who gave its name to the most prominent city in Washington, formerly known as New York, declared to European negotiators: 'All parts of this land are sacred'].

23 *Essais sur les modernes* (Gallimard, 1964).

A Supplement to the White Man's Burden

Lobo Antunes, History, the Colonial Wars, and the April Revolution

Luís Madureira

in *Portuguese Literary and Cultural Studies* 19/20 (2011): 227–46.
Excerpts translated by Bruno Zhu.

Abstract This essay opens with an examination of Portuguese novels about the colonial wars which seek to expose the referential emptiness of the Salazarist imperial mystique, and present its "civilizing mission" as an example of the very un-Historicity which Hegel notoriously ascribes to Africa. Such texts arguably employ "postcolonial" strategies of reading empire. It is precisely this gesture that Lobo Antunes refuses to perform. His fiction suggests that to try to link the protagonist's colonial story with Angola's narrative of resistance would only confirm his complicity with the colonial project. By the same token, the April Revolution appears bereft of historical meaning, reduced to one in an infinite chain of exchangeable signifiers mobilized to name a desire for totality that cannot but fall short of its object. In Antunes's fiction, Portugal's quest for universality seems as illusory as the *estadonovista* yearning for the resurgence of an etiolated imperial glory.

In an early chapter of Günter Grass's *Tin Drum*, Oskar Matzerath, the novel's narrator, expresses a characteristically neurotic desire: "I wish I could be a toasty warm brick, constantly exchanged for myself, lying beneath my grandmother's skirts" (147). To repeat the question Oskar attributes to his implied reader: "What [...] can Oskar be after beneath his grandmother's skirts? Oblivion, a home, the ultimate Nirvana?" Oskar's answer is as pointed as it is startling: "Afrika suchte ich unter den Röcken" [("I was looking for Africa under the skirts")[1] (*Tin Drum* 125)] (*Blechtrommel* 147):

> This was the watershed, he continues, the union of all streams; here special winds blew, or else there was no wind at all; dry and warm, you could listen to the whistling of the rain; here ships made fast or weighed anchors [...] beneath my grandmother's skirts it was always summer [...]. Nowhere could I have been more at peace with the calendar than beneath my grandmother's skirts. (126)

Oskar may be paraphrasing here a Baudelairean wish to be here [*da*], there [*là-bas]*, and nowhere—or anywhere out of this world [*n'importe où hors du monde*]. Like Baudelaire's oneirical land, the place beneath the grandmother's skirts is a paradoxical true fiction ("un vrai pays de Cocagne"), the uncharted harbor where numinous ships come to slumber at the end of parabolic journeys to Infinity, "un de ces pays qui sont les analogies de la Mort" ["one of those countries that are the analogies of Death"]; a place at once exotic and familiar: *l'Orient de l'Occident, la Chine de l'Europe* (Baudelaire 107, 179). It is an uncanny topos that turns out to be the common "entrance to the former *Heim* [home] of all human beings, to the place where each one of us lived once upon a time and 'in the beginning'" (Freud, "Uncanny" 146). As Oskar later confesses, his "aim is to get back to the umbilical cord; that is the sole purpose behind this whole vast verbal effort" (179). About the "Uncanny" (or *unheimlich*) Freud has famously argued that the prefix *un* serves as "the token of repression," of something familiar (or *heimlich*) which has been repressed.

For instance, "whenever a man dreams of a place or country and says to himself, while he is still dreaming, 'this place is familiar to me, I've been here before,'' we may interpret the place as being his mother's genitals or her body" ("Uncanny" 146). The Uncanny, then, "occurs either when infantile complexes which have been repressed are once more revived by some impression, or when primitive beliefs which have been surmounted seem once more to be confirmed" (150). Ironically, inasmuch as Oskar's "uncanny" life story is defined by a willed resurgence of childhood traumas, of the revenants of a primitive ancestry, as it were, it parallels the very politico-historical itinerary from which he so obstinately seeks to distance himself.

Oskar's drive to replicate the undifferentiated and ceramic recurrence of the Same shares in common with the Nazi project its barbaric gloss of the distinctively modern desire to obliterate the old order. In both instances, the new departure turns out to be a return, and the point of origin is so radically original that it dwells outside of historical (or calendar) time altogether. It lies beyond the "origin" itself. Oskar's desire to reach the primal stasis of a perennially embryonic mode of being can thus be said to relate to the modern as Freud's "compulsion to repeat" does to the pleasure principle: it is "something that seems more primitive, more elementary, more instinctual, and which ends up overriding [the latter]" (*Pleasure Principle* 25). Insofar as it is an "unconscious mental process," it is unaffected by time. Indeed, the idea of time is completely alien to it. Oskar's instinct to restore an earlier state of things is, in this psychoanalytical sense, "the expression of the inertia inherent in organic life [...] of the *conservative* nature of living substance" (*Pleasure Principle* 43).

And this "initial state from which the living entity has at one time or another departed and to which it is striving to return by the circuitous paths along which its development leads" is of course death: a return to an inorganic existence immanent in the organism itself, the embodiment of its wish "to die only in its own fashion"[1] (*Pleasure Principle* 45, 47). In this sense, Oskar's *Afrika* becomes not only an analogy of death, but the figure for a wholesale civilizational collapse, for a cultural disposition "to give a deceptive appearance of being [a] force tending towards change and progress, whilst in fact [it] is merely seeking to reach an ancient goal by paths alike old and new" (*Pleasure Principle* 45). If one assumes, as one of *Tin Drum*'s possible tropological frameworks, Freud's assertion of the striking similarity between "the process of civilization and the libidinal development of the individual" (*Civilization* 51), then Oskar's obsessive desire to return to the uterine tropics suggests that the titanic battle between Eros and Thanatos, between the instinct of life and the instinct of destruction to which the evolution of civilization may be reduced according to Freud (*Civilization* 82), culminates with the absolute victory of the latter—with a retrocession into a primitive state in which "man" knows no restrictions to his savage instincts.

It is as though the absolute "end of History," which Europe signifies for Hegel (*History* 103), the principle of "self-conscious Reason" which defines the occident's epistemological impetus "to take back into itself, into its unitary nature" (*Mind* 45), the recalcitrant and protean alterity of the world confronting it; as though the "development and realization of freedom" which European civilization putatively embodies were to retrogress not just to the beginning of History, but to its "threshold," the Unhistorical and Undeveloped netherworld to which Hegel consigns Africa in *The Philosophy of History*. It is as though, in intimating that "the nation lives the same kind of life as the individual," Grass wishes simultaneously to underscore a crucial "Hegelian" distinction between these two processes. In the case of the nation, "death appears to imply destruction by its own agency" (*History* 75).

This is the peculiar eschatology that appears to govern the plots of several recent (or "post-revolutionary") novels about Portugal's African wars. Hence, although in a very broad sense these narratives may certainly be classified as twentieth-century "adaptations" of Joseph Conrad's great Africanist novella, they nonetheless purportedly succeed in transcending what the late Edward Said has called its tragic limitation, that is, the fact that "even though [Conrad] could see clearly that on one level imperialism was essentially pure dominance and land-grabbing, he could not then conclude that imperialism had to end so that the 'natives' could lead lives free from European domination" (30). By contrast, it is precisely this recognition that lays the epistemological ground for Portugal's latter-day novelistic journeys into a stereotypical "heart of darkness." In this light, the renowned cartographic blank upon which little Marlow's desire is inscribed ("when I grow up I will go there" [33]) turns out to be disquietingly self-reflexive. Like the hankering of the perennially and "willfully" diminutive Oskar for a matricial *Afrika*, Marlow's wish to "go there" is in the last instance a death wish, a desire to destroy, "in [his] own fashion" (*Pleasure Principle* 47), the culture and civilization that ultimately enable him to define himself as a human subject. By dint of an impossible return "to the earliest beginnings of the earth," to "a prehistoric earth" (Conrad 59, 62)—to the threshold of History in the Hegelian sense—both the young Marlow and Oskar strive to follow in reverse order the developmental itinerary that the West's particularist and fabular "universal history" has charted.

The Nazi project reproduces at the national level this *viaje a la semilla*, as Alejo Carpentier would call it, this return voyage to the infant stage. It initiates the backward movement across history's great epochs that, rather than culminating in the German spirit's "blissful self-rediscovery," as Nietzsche once exuberantly foretold (96), leads, in the words of the narrator-protagonist of Carpentier's *Lost Steps*, to the brutal interruption of the West's emancipatory narrative,[2] to an absolute modernity which is at the same time a kind of civilizational death fugue: "What was new here, unprecedented [*inédito*], modern, was that cavern of horrors, that ministry of horror [...] in which everything bore witness to torture, mass extermination, crematories" (Carpentier 94). Similarly, the "anticolonial" appropriations of Hegel's master/slave dialectic, exemplified in the writings of Frantz Fanon, Aimé Césaire, and C. L. R. James, among many others, suggest that the "master race," in dehumanizing those with "a different complexion or slightly flatter noses," ultimately dehumanizes itself. As the template to Nazism's genocidal procedures, colonialism, Césaire asserts in his *Discours sur le colonialisme*, becomes *la négation pure et simple de la civilisation*. As a consequence, the "white world" reveals itself "horribly weary from its immense efforts / its stiff joints [cracking] under the hard stars" (69).

From the early twentieth century onward, "anti-colonial" literatures endeavor variously to rewrite this imputed civilizational death-instinct as the opening—the *blank space*, as it were—upon which, in Gayatri Spivak's terms, "a new magisterium [may] construct itself [from the West's "magisterial texts"] in the name of the Other" (*Critique* 7). It is putatively this wholesale collapse of European civilization, and its attendant notions of progress, enlightenment, and reason that Conrad's novella foreshadows as well. Only in this rather restricted sense would I be willing to go along with Alfred J. López's provocative claim that Conrad's novella produces "an opening into the postcolonial" (59). Grounding his own reading of *Heart of Darkness* on Guyana's Wilson Harris's designation of the text as a "frontier" novel, López argues that Conrad's narrative clears the space in which postcolonial literature was later to emerge. For López, then, the novel betokens "a capacity, in the most general terms, for language—or more specifically, for a discourse with the [...] capability of representing *difference*" (46).

It is a similar "tampering" with the authority of "Europe's long story" that Spivak identifies as one of the specifically postcolonial strategies of engaging with the West's powerful and enduring narrative (*Teaching* 75). It seems to be in this disruptive spirit as well that the Portuguese critic Eduardo Lourenço, writing in the throes of the precipitate decolonization unleashed in the aftermath of Portugal's 1974 revolution, reduces to *nothing* the impact on the national *psyche* of the vertiginous collapse of a 500-year old colonial empire: "Mas marcas duradouras na alma de quem 'teve' quinhentos anos de império *nada*, ou só a ficção encarecente que n'*Os Lusíadas* ecoa, não como mudadora da sua alma, mas como simples *nomenclatura* extasiada de terras e lugares que na verdade, salvo Goa, nunca habitámos como senhores delas" (*Labirinto* 43).[3] [I]

More recently, Lourenço has spoken of Portugal's "puro império de sonho,"[II] describing its late nineteenth-century colonial enterprise in Africa as "a nossa fuga simbólica para o imaginário imperial" (*Mitologia* 130).[III] Recent metropolitan narratives about Portugal's colonial wars seek consciously (at times even programmatically) to elaborate as a discursive "capacity" the link with the postcolonial that both López and Harris regard as a potentiality in Conrad's narrative discourse, and which Edward Said considers absent from it.[4] They therefore attempt to recode what Eduardo Lourenço defines as a historiographic *nothing* as a metropolitan version of the very negation of History that Hegel notoriously imputes to Africa. Death in these war novels emerges as the unconscious wish not only of the colonial subject but of the metropolis itself. The backwardness or marginality that, in the eyes of several of the leaders of Africa's liberation struggles, belied even the pretense of a Portuguese "civilizing mission" would thus appear to be confirmed by this contemporary recurrence of an ostensible desire for the end of empire, a death-drive which, as I argue elsewhere, can already be glimpsed in the interstices of Portugal's sixteenth-century discourses of maritime expansion.[5]

I 'Yet deep scars in the soul of someone who 'had' five hundred years of empire are nowhere, only the overwrought fiction echoed by Os Lusíadas, not to change his soul, but solely as mesmerising nomenclature for lands and places that in reality, except Goa, we never were lords of'

II 'pure dream empire'

III 'our symbolic exit into the imperial imaginary'

In António Lobo Antunes's *As naus*,[6] just as in Manuel Alegre's *Jornada de África* (1989) and João de Melo's *Autópsia de um mar em ruínas* (1984), this putative death-wish functions explicitly as the synecdoche of metropolitan disintegration. In Alegre's *Jornada*, this link is established with a sustained set of allusions to the conveniently metonymic death of King Sebastian I. As Alegre asserts in a poem written at least a decade before *Jornada* was published,

> Alcácer Quibir foi sempre o passado por dentro do presente
> [...]
> Quinhentos anos dentro destes anos
> Alcácer Quibir [é] este fantasma sobre a nossa idade
> [...]
> [É] ir morrer além do mar por coisa nenhuma
> [...] um tempo parado no tempo [...]
> Porque um fantasma é rei de Portugal. (n.p.)[IV]

IV 'Alcácer Quibir was always the past within the present
[...]
Five hundred years within these years
Alcácer Quibir [is] the ghost of our age
[...]
[It is] to die across the sea for nothing
[...]
paused time within time [...]
Since a ghost is the king of Portugal. (n.p.)'

V 'the queer king'

VI 'a blond teen, with a crown on his head and sullen cheeks, coming from Alcácer Quibir with copper bangles made by the gypsies of Carcavelos and white chokers from Tangier on his neck'

Similarly, in António Lobo Antunes's *As naus*, the ghost of King Sebastian haunts the entire narrative, as does the attendant threat of a Castilian invasion, of the country's untimely yet foretold death. At the end of the novel, in an obsessive-compulsive reenactment of the closing section of Pessoa's *Mensagem*, the returnees from a collapsing empire, ravaged by mental illness and tropical diseases, gather (like "a band of robed seagulls" ["um bando de gaivotas em roupão" (247)]) on the beach at Ericeira. Their aim is to prepare for the arrival of the Fifth Empire's ghostly harbinger: "o rei maricas" (241),[V] "um adolescente loiro, de coroa na cabeça e beiços amuados, vindo de Alcácer Quibir com pulseiras de cobre trabalhado dos ciganos de Carcavelos e colares baratos de Tânger ao pescoço" (247).[VI] Like King Sebastian, and indeed the *estadonovista* imperial mystique, these "dying colonialists" apparently suffer from the quixotic affliction as defined by Foucault. Their delusional efforts to decipher in Renaissance discourses of expansion a redemptive resemblance to Portugal's present-day imperialism, their stubborn insistence to read those ancient chronicles and its "rotting" twentieth-century avatar as belonging to the same hallowed text, verge also "upon the visionary or madness" (Foucault 47).

Ultimately, Salazarist colonial discourses also "have [no] value apart from the slender fiction which they represent" (Foucault 48). They are, in this way (and to borrow Eduardo Lourenço's sardonic definition of the Portuguese), "more Quixotic than Don Quixote" (*Mitologia* 14). At the end of *As naus*, the only thing the lugubrious group of ex-colonials is able to descry is expectedly "the ocean, empty as far as the line of the horizon." They remain nonetheless the willing prisoners of a kind of imperial sublime, "aguardando, ao som de uma flauta que as vísceras do mar emudeciam, os relinchos de um cavalo impossível" (247),[VII] performing the tenuous hope, already inscribed in the *Lusíadas*' invocation, that the willful young king would restore the decaying sixteenth-century empire to its former resplendent glory. In this restricted sense, Antunes's narrative fits Adorno's description of contemporary novels as "negative epics [:] testimonials to a state of affairs in which the individual liquidates himself" (35).

VII 'waiting, for the sound of a flute engulfed in the bowels of the sea, the neighing of an impossible horse'

In Melo's *Autópsia de um mar em ruínas*, the fascist desire to restore the grandeur of Portugal's sixteenth-century empire is gradually refigured as a repetition-compulsion, a collective drive to return to a historical "womb" whose culmination is unavoidably death: "cada um procurava a segurança [...] um ninho onde esse corpo à beira da fragmentação pudesse ter ainda a ilusão de regressar ao óvulo e ao seio da mãe" (13), "e eis a morte [...]. O ar tornou[-se] gordo como a placenta onde fui gerado," "vai morrer um homem. Vai morrer um país que matou um milhão e quinhentos mil homens na guerra" (292, 293).[VIII] Yet both *Jornada* and *Autópsia* seek to move considerably beyond the mere chronicling of an imperial death foretold. They apparently subscribe to the compensatory political posture which, according to Lourenço, Portugal adopts in response to a traumatizing decolonization: "o que perdíamos em espaço e em riqueza potencial (e real) era compensado pela *exemplaridade revolucionária*, ou sobretudo, por uma exemplaridade *democrática* que tinha o condão de nos subtrair do lote das nações retrógradas politicamente e nos conciliar a benevolência e estima do universo" (*Labirinto* 49).[IX]

VIII 'each of them looked for safety [...] a refuge where their bodies coming apart could still believe in the illusion of returning to the egg and the breasts of their mother", "and thus death [...]. The air thickened resembling the placenta that bore me," "a man will die. A country that killed one million and five hundred thousand men in war will die'

IX 'what we were losing in scale and in potential (and real) riches was being compensated by the revolutionary exemplary, most importantly, by a democratic exemplary that could remove us from the list of politically backward nations and reconcile with the benevolence and recognition of the universe'

As Lourenço has proposed more recently, "read in reverse" (*lido às avessas*) the "disaster" that the dissolution of the Portuguese colonial empire constituted "se converteu no acto fundador da Nova Democracia portuguesa" (*Mitologia* 139).[X] Along similar lines, Alegre and Melo attempt to adumbrate what Paul Gilroy designates "the inversion of the relationship between margin and centre as it has appeared within the master discourses of the master race" (45) a reversal, which as C. L. R. James asserts, is embodied in the peculiar circumstances surrounding the collapse of Portugal's colonial empire:

X 'converted itself into the foundation of Portuguese New Democracy'

> Portugal which dominated areas of Africa for 500 years has not only lost control over them; but the revolutionary developments in Africa have affected the future of Portugal itself. In other words, the movement is in the opposite direction—instead of movements from Europe stimulating revolutionary developments in Africa, liberation struggles in Africa have unleashed movements of tremendous importance in Europe itself. (378)

It is this remarkable alteration of the trajectory which Hegel imposes on universal history that Melo's and Alegre's novels attempt to register. As in Césaire's "Notebook of a Return to My Native Land," the death of the metropolis prefigures the "birth" of a new humanity in Africa: "cabeças de homens brancos caem degoladas por cada golpe; seus pescoços antecipadamente condenados pelo dia grande que vai chegar ainda" (Melo 123).[XI]

XI 'heads of white men fly from each stroke; their necks already doomed by the glorious day yet to come'

In Lobo Antunes's *Os cus de Judas* (1979), the narrator-protagonist foresees the impending demise of his European homeland exactly in the ritual dances of "um povo cuja inesgotável vitalidade [ele] entrevira já, anos antes, no trompete solar de Louis Armstrong, expulsando a neurastenia e o azedume com a alegria musculosa do seu canto" (58),[XII] in the inflections of a "esquisita linguagem que eu entendia mal, mas se aparentava ao saxofone de Charlie Parker quando não grita o seu ódio ferido pelo mundo cruel e ridículo dos brancos" (181).[7] [XIII] This glimpse of a world which the narrator of *Os cus*

XII 'a folk whose endless vitality [he had] already glimpsed, years before, in Louis Armstrong's trumpet, banishing the weariness and bitterness with the muscular joy of his singing'

XIII 'awkward language that I barely understood, but it reappeared in Charlie Parker's saxophone whenever it wasn't screaming in pain, hurling hatred to the cruel and ridiculous White world'

places under the sign of authenticity not only glosses Langston Hughes's "Trumpet Player," but it repeats a cultural opposition pervasive in *négritude* poetry.[8] Here, too, the vibrancy and vitality of the African world reflects back to the European narrator the inauthenticity and morbidity of his own culture: "sentia-me melancolicamente herdeiro de um velho país desajeitado e agonizante, de uma Europa repleta de furúnculos de palácios de pedras de bexiga de catedrais" (58).[XIV]

By the same token, the chapters from Melo's novel that focus on Angola's anti-colonial resistance adhere to Sartre's postulate regarding the universality of any individual (existential) project: "Every project, even that of a Chinese, an Indian or a Negro, can be understood by a European [who] can redo in himself the project of the Chinese, the Indian or the African [...] as long as [s/ he] has sufficient information [*renseignements suffisants*]" (69–70). Falling prey perhaps to the "Eurocentric arrogance" that Spivak ascribes to Sartre's assertion (*Critique* 173), Melo attempts to incorporate, as a counterpoint to his own account of a metropolitan death, the Angolans' project of liberation, the latter's subterranean (and subcutaneous) narration of a nation yet to be born: "a história da libertação [...] escrita com sangue na memória do povo" (305), "essas histórias que ficavam escritas na terra-mãe [das quais] a pátria se fazia no tempo" (119).[XV] Melo's *Autópsia* seeks not only to undermine dominant Portuguese colonial discourses but to reproduce, or at least gesture toward, Angola's incipient nationalist project.

XIV 'I felt wistful being the heir of a worn out country, cumbersome and dying, of a Europe crammed with stone palaces cluttered with cathedrals'

XV 'a liberation story [...] etched in blood onto people's memory", "the kind of stories that were written in the soil [of which] a country was made of'

In his effort to establish a causal link between the death of the metropolis and the birth of a new Angolan nation, to interject an emergent "counternarration" into the fabric of his own narrative of imperial decadence, Melo thus exhibits that "revolutionary exemplariness" which Eduardo Lourenço ironically brands as a compensation for the empire's loss—an exemplariness that in a sense supplements "the white man's burden." What distinguishes this supplementary mediation from the one Derrida describes is not just its "self-consciousness" but its expressed desire to take the place of the very term—colonialism—it defers. This is precisely the exemplary gesture which Lobo Antunes's narrative refuses to perform. Other than the phantasmal guerrillas, the central figure of resistance in *Os cus de Judas* is the narrator's African lover Sofia, an MPLA operative who is gang-raped and subsequently murdered by a PIDE station chief: "mulher liberta que nenhum pide, nenhum tropa, nenhum cipaio calaria" (187).[XVI]

XVI 'a free woman that no state spy, no soldier, no policeman could silence'

The narrator's involvement with her is in fact the one facet of his Angolan experience that he deliberately conceals from his interlocutor. He invokes Sofia's image, her "triumphant laughter" ["gargalhada vitoriosa"], but nevertheless refuses to transcribe her words, turning instead to his own pusillanimous silence before her extra-judicial execution: "saio deste aquário de azulejos como saí do quartel da pide [...] sem a coragem de um grito de indignação ou revolta, a acabar de cumprir esta noite como outrora cumpri, sem protestar, vinte e sete meses de escravidão sangrenta" (192–3).[XVII] The narrator's refusal to tell Sofia's story, his insistence on guarding her secret, stands in direct contrast to the PIDE agent's brutal tactics of interrogation. It stops short of reproducing what Spivak calls "the ethnocentric and reverse-ethnocentric double-bind" (that is, converting the native into the object of an "enthusiastic information-retrieval") (*Critique* 118). In this way, Sofia marks the site of an irretrievable alterity, of the novel's inaccessible exterior. She represents a diegetic limit beyond which Antunes's narration cannot proceed without reproducing the very violence and terror which it sets out to displace.

XVII 'I leave this tiled chamber just how I left the headquarters of PIDE [...] too weak to shout in anger or outrage, and carry this night like I've done before, without protest, twenty seven months of bloody bondage'

The silent acquiescence of Antunes' narrator to Sofia's torture and assassination, as well as his resigned collaboration with the *Estado Novo*'s counterinsurgent campaign inevitably render him complicit with the colonial project he abhors. Any endeavor to incorporate the subterranean idiom of resistance (the struggle for which Sofia sacrifices herself) into his own (metropolitan) account of the colonial war would only exacerbate this complicity. It would, in effect, inscribe itself in the history of "the arrogance of the radical European humanist conscience, which will consolidate itself by imagining the other... through the collection of information" (Spivak, *Critique* 171). In this way, *Os cus de Judas* sets itself apart both from Melo's *Autópsia* and Alegre's *Jornada*, which, in a broad sense, both endeavor to exhume a subterranean similitude between the colonial troops and the nationalist guerrillas. Rather than signal the double emancipation putatively unleashed by the abrupt fall of the colonial empire, Antunes's narrative of the colonial war annuls the utopian promise of April '74. The remarkable public silence that greets the empire's collapse in *Os cus de Judas*, the "unparalleled" absence of even a vestigial traumatic sign on the "national psyche," the collective refusal to rethink "*[n]a sua totalidade [a] nossa imagem perante nós mesmos e no espelho do mundo*" (Lourenço, Labirinto 45; italics in the original),[XVIII] marks the ineluctable closure of the revolutionary cycle. "Se a revolução acabou, e em certo sentido acabou de facto, é porque os mortos de África, de boca cheia de terra, não podem protestar, e hora a hora a direita os vai matando, de novo, e nós, os sobreviventes, continuamos duvidosos de estar vivos" (Antunes, *Cus* 73).[XIX]

XVIII 'in its totality our image for ourselves reflected in the mirror of the world'

XIX 'If the revolution ended, and in many ways it did, it's because the dead in Africa, with their mouths full of dust, can't protest, and hour by hour the right carries on killing them, yet again, while us, the survivors, doubt whether we are still alive'

Not only is the radical temporal rift which divides the metropolis from its colonial "dependencies" during the armed struggle not transcended by the April revolution, but, as Antunes's later fiction suggests, Portugal's historical "stagnation" appears only to intensify in the post-revolutionary period. The inversion in the motion of History, which C. L. R. James views as inextricably linked to "liberation struggles in Africa," manifests itself in the metropolis as a lingering "backwardness," as an effective reversal of the stereotyped hierarchical relationship between Europe and the "dark continent." Small wonder, therefore, that in Antunes's sixth novel, *Auto dos danados*, the third in a quartet whose last installment is *As naus*, a back-packing German couple, who "invade" a curio shop in the southern Portuguese province of Alentejo in the wake of the revolution, examine "as loiças e as peles, como os navegadores antigos as estatuetas de pau-santo dos pretos,"[XX] insisting on regarding even the most trivial act as some "ritual primitivo, executado em sua honra por um membro da tribo" (250, 251).[XXI] In a general sense, the scene epitomizes the contradictory position Portugal occupies in relation to the "developed" world at the moment of decolonization. In the words of Boaventura de Sousa Santos:

XX 'the tableware and hides, like how old sailors used to with rosewood figurines made by blacks'

XXI 'primitive ritual, performed in their honour by a tribesman'

> Portugal was the center in relation to its colonies and the periphery in relation to [post-industrial Europe]. In less technical terms, we can say that for a long time Portugal was simultaneously a colonizing and a colonized country. On April 25 1974, Portugal was the least developed country in Europe and at the same time the sole possessor of the largest and longest-lasting European colonial empire. (105)

In *Fado alexandrino* (1983), perhaps Antunes's most full-fledged attempt to novelize the historical articulation between the disintegration of the colonial empire and the April revolution, the "unthinkable" desire to convert Portugal into a European Cuba (Lourenço, *Labirinto* 50) appears ultimately to produce a (historically) *necessary* displacement of the former metropolis into the margins of world history. The historical vacuum purportedly defining Portugal's anachronistic imperialism is "superceded" in *Fado* by a post-colonial collapse of the historical which, on the face of it, recalls the slippage of History into parodic repetition undergirding Marx's famous account of France's 1848 Revolution (*The 18th Brumaire of Louis Napoleon*). The absence of historicity that was Portugal under fascism now comes to determine, indeed "overdetermine" its revolutionary phase. The novel, which relates the gathering of five veterans of the Mozambican front in a Lisbon restaurant to commemorate the tenth anniversary of their battalion's return to the metropole in 1973, suggests that the April Revolution is as original as the title's *fado alexandrino*. It resembles a melodramatic national (and nationalist) ballad corseted into the narrative counterpart of the twelve-syllable neo-classical verse revived by French and Portuguese Romanticists alike. *Fado alexandrino* is therefore neatly divided into three parts of *twelve* chapters each.

In such a context, the Revolution becomes but the latest *fado* that the deluded nation croons to itself, the most recent wish-fantasy to replace the fascist imperial mystique. Or, borrowing Eduardo Lourenço's terms, April 25, 1974 signals the hasty reinvention of a "new mythology" (*Mitologia* 147). It marks a political instance of the Uncanny, an apparent revival and confirmation of repressed infantile complexes and primitive beliefs: "voltamos, quase sem transição, senão aos 'antigos tempos,' aos mesmos caseiros e deliciosos negócios públicos, instituídos pouco a pouco como uma festa permanente" (*Mitologia* 147).[XXII] In accordance with this structure of repetition, the *Estado Novo*'s "construção mítica da imagem de um *Portugal-menino-jesus-das-nações* [...] 'eón' histórico predestinado à *regeneração espiritual do universo*" (Lourenço, *Labirinto* 39)[XXIII] would be at once supplanted and repeated in the "imagem de um *Portugal revolucionário*, exemplo inicial e iniciático de uma subversão democrática da ordem capitalista europeia, [que fazia] confluir para um povo sem espaço para um tal sonho os fantasmas da esquerda europeia que triunfava no Alentejo e na Lisnave por procuração" (*Labirinto* 49).[XXIV]

To be sure, this new mythic model of national regeneration was "de vocação não apenas revolucionária mas universalista" (*Mitologia* 147).[XXV] For, as the communications officer, *Fado's* most militant revolutionary, drunkenly confesses:

> O que nós pretendíamos era uma verdadeira sublevação popular conduzida pelos camponeses, pela classe operária, pelos oprimidos em geral, a caminho de um socialismo absoluto [...]. Acreditei na revolução, na queda da burguesia, na próxima, iminente vitória final da classe operária [...]. E ocupava-me a imaginar ardentemente [...] a imorredoira classe operária a subir a Avenida num frenesim de hinos e bandeiras, dependurando impiedosamente dos candeeiros os sociais-democratas, os patrões, os polícias, e os lacaios do Capital, e proclamando, na Rotunda, o Marxismo-Leninismo-Maoismo [...]. [Erguíamos] o paraíso da autêntica democracia popular na Europa apodrecida. (166, 415, 417)[XXVI]

XXII 'we return, almost seamlessly, to the 'old times,' to the simple and familiar issues that creep back slowly like a never-ending show'

XXIII 'mythical construct of the *baby-Jesus-of-all-nations Portugal* [...] the historical 'eon' predestined to cause the *spiritual renewal of the universe*'

XXIV 'the image of a revolutionary Portugal, a prime and aspirational example of a democratic subversion within the European capitalist order, bringing the ghosts of the European Left that had already gripped Alentejo and Lisnave, to folk without space for such a dream'

XXV 'a calling that was not only revolutionary but also universalist'

What is farcical about this revolutionary fantasy is its belated belief that a "petit-bourgeois coup" (166) could serve as the original "model for a democratic subversion of the European capitalist order" (*Labirinto* 45). The anachronism of Portugal's revolutionary project ends up both displacing and reproducing the very terms of its anachronistic colonial enterprise: "as eternamente malogradas tentativas de alfabetizar os bairros da lata no intuito [...] de converter ["operários indiferentes"], como os missionários de África aos pretinhos prometidos ao inferno, ao Marxismo-Leninismo-

XXVI 'What we wanted was a real populist rebellion waged by peasants, by the working class, by the oppressed in general, towards total socialism [...]. I believed in the revolution, in the fall of the bourgeoisie, in the near, imminent victory of the working class [...]. And I stayed busy picturing [...] the undying working class marching up the Avenida in a frenzy of anthems and flags, ruthlessly hanging from the streetlamp the social-democrats, the bosses, the policemen, and the lackeys of Capital, while chanting at the Rotunda [...]. [We'd give rise to] an authentic grassroots democracy in the midst of a rotten Europe.'

XXVII 'the protracted attempts to teach the slums how to read in order to [...] convert them ["indifferent workers"], just like how missionaries in Africa used to do to the doomed little black kids, to the Marxism-Leninism-Maoism and save them from the terrifying capitalist purgatory'

XXVIII 'the authentic grassroots democratic utopia in a rotten Europe that is unliveable, polluted by coca-cola, disposable lighters and chewing gums, plagued by cancerous multinationals and the heinous exploitation of liberal economy'

XXIX 'The entire country awaits for our righteous and vital liberating act'

XXX 'Such a stubborn little prick, Artur, sighed the cloud of perfume while doubling down on it, the more I kiss it the shyer it gets, that mischievous little prick.'

XXXI 'the misery and the evil of war"—"a flag hung from its pole resembling a limp penis", "Salazar ["the Cuck"] stuck his finger, probably the only thing he ever stuck with, into", "eunuch ministers," "ministerial eunuchs'

XXXII 'a phoney revolution'. 'There was no revolution'

Maoismo salvador do tenebroso purgatório capitalista" (*Fado* 425).[XXVII] And like the discarded notion of the "civilizing mission," the Revolution becomes a fetish, the fetish with which incongruously vehement militants endeavor to combat the fetishism of the commodity: "o paraíso da autêntica democracia popular na Europa apodrecida, sordidamente invivível, poluída pela coca-cola, os isqueiros de atirar fora e as pastilhas elásticas, minada pelo cancro das multinacionais e pela exploração infame da economia liberal" (417).[XXVIII]

The Revolution in Antunes's *Fado* thus assumes its place in a metonymic chain of "inappropriate" and partial objects which "serve to symbolize the most profound lost object" (Lacan 198). It is endlessly displaced, deferred, only to emerge in a different guise. But it always and ineluctably signifies the lack that structures (revolutionary) desire: "What [the subject] is trying to see [...] is the object as absence. What [he] is looking for and finds is merely a shadow, a shadow behind the curtain. There he will phantasize any magic of presence [...]. What he is looking for is not [...] the phallus—but precisely its absence" (Lacan 182). Among the complex and imbricated narrative strands which make up the structure of *Fado alexandrino*, two contrapuntal phrases stand out in this respect. The first is an urgent whisper by one of the novel's several farcical revolutionaries reported in the communications officer's account of a failed and vaudevillesque left-wing coup: "O país inteiro aguarda de nós esta justa e imprescindível acção libertadora" (*Fado* 431).[XXIX] The meaningful rejoinder to this revolutionary wish-fantasy comes from the colonel's concurrent and desultory narration of his agonizing courtship with his future wife, in the form of the following entreaty: "Mas que teimosa a sua torneirinha está, Artur, comentou a nuvem de perfume redobrando o zelo, a marota quantos mais bejinhos lhe dou mais minguada fica" (*Fado* 431).[XXX]

The very same object that in *Os cus de Judas* signified "miséria e a maldade da Guerra"—"a bandeira pendente do seu mastro idêntica a um pénis sem força" (199), "Salazar ["o *Capado*"] espetava o dedo, única coisa, decerto, que ele alguma vez espetou" (76), "eunucos ministros," "ministros eunucos" (129),[XXXI] etc.—resurfaces in *Fado* as the signifier of the Revolution, or rather of its obsessively made-up absence. In effect, the consensus about 25 April 1974 is precisely that it never rises above the level of what the communications officer calls "uma revolução de chacha" (166). "Não houve revolução nenhuma" (480),[XXXII] the private, the novel's only proletarian character, concludes: "Não houve uma revolta a sério, os que mandavam antes ocupam o poleiro outra vez [...] de forma que continuamos na mesma terra de merda" (224); "a mesma inalterável, melancólica, estreita paisagem em que apenas se cabe apertado e de pé" (505), "e esta merda sempre igual a esta merda" (541).[XXXIII] To go by what the second lieutenant affirms, this is the very same shit, it seems, that is emblematic of the fascist state. For if the anal drive, as Lacan indicates, is the domain of oblativity, of the gift, then the surfeit of human waste that is Portugal's colonial war in *Os cus de Judas* compensates in the last instance for all the lacks (e.g., the "absence of History") which the regime has failed consistently to make good.

XXXIII 'There was no real revolution, the ones in power before are still there [...] so we are still in the same shithole"; "the same unchanged, sad, flimsy landscape where you only fit if you're tied up and standing", "this shit being the same shit'

As a "gigantic" lieutenant beseeches the protagonist of *Os cus de Judas* "in a little boy's voice": "Doutor arranje-me a tal doença antes que eu rebente aqui na estrada da merda que tenho dentro"[XXXIV] (154); and the narrator himself later exclaims, "trazíamos vinte e cinco meses de guerra nas tripas, vinte e cinco meses de comer merda, e beber merda, e lutar por merda, e adoecer por merda, e cair por merda" (211); "passámos vinte e sete meses nos cus de Judas [na] mesma merda" (241).[XXXV] Excrement is all that the State, and its postrevolutionary dejecta, can offer its citizens in lieu of what it ought to have accorded them: democracy, freedom, human rights. To paraphrase Lacan once again, it is at the anal level that the fascist government inscribes itself "in its morality (*dans sa morale*)" (104). When, as a result of the gaping hole at its core, the *Estado Novo* is caught egregiously short even of its own paltry objectives, the only thing it can give its subjects is precisely shit. Rather than Hegel's Idea, then, what the *Estado Novo* "ethically embodies" is ultimately shit as well. "É curioso como tudo se tornou tão depressa como antes do golpe" (638),[XXXVI] the second lieutenant in *Fado alexandrino* laments, thus alluding to the very same *nothing*, the negation of History that, in the Portuguese war novels mentioned above, figures the Salazarist regime's absolute lack of progress or development.

XXXIV 'Doctor, find me that sickness before I blow up in this shit motorway I have inside me'

XXXV 'we were carrying twenty five months of war in our guts, twenty five months of eating shit, of drinking shit, of fighting for shit, of getting sick because of shit, of falling over shit"; "we spent twenty seven months in God's forsaken land in the same shit'

XXXVI 'It's funny how everything turned back to the way it was before the coup'

Not only does this absence of History return to determine what José Saramago in *História do cerco de Lisboa* terms the Revolution's inaugural *yes*, but it has reemerged as the lack that structures and engenders desire itself. As with the "Purloined Letter" in Lacan's famous reading of Poe's detective story, it is not for a specific revolutionary signified—for instance, the authentic revolutionary *content* which Marx predicts will necessarily go *beyond the phrase*; it is not for the Revolution's signified that *Fado*'s characters yearn. Rather, it is their closeness to the Revolution as signifier which appears to determine them as subjects. What the April Revolution means is thus at once everything and nothing, either "the most profound lost object," or, "the object as absence" (Lacan 198, 182). And the fullness or emptiness of its meaning depends precisely on each character's perceived proximity to it.

As the colonel muses in reply to the private's outraged question whether the Revolution was nothing but "os trutas a engolirem-se uns aos outros, à bulha, a ver quem se amanhava melhor" (*Fado* 317)[XXXVII]:

XXXVII 'the smartarses talking over each other, pushing around, to see who could do better'

> Não a revolução nem os que fizeram a revolução mas os vorazes micróbios cancerosos que dela se alimentavam e em torno dela se moviam, partidos políticos, jogos de influências, ódios pessoais, as insaciáveis ambiçõesinhas dos frustrados: quero ser marechal, quero ser rico [...] quero um barco, uma casa com piscina, uma televisão a cores, uma amante cara [...] quero lixar os outros, quero esmigalhar os outros, quero enrabar os outros, quero ficar sozinho, heróico e de bronze, no cimo vertiginoso do pedestal. (317)[XXXVIII]

XXXVIII 'Neither the revolution, nor the ones who carried it, but the feisty and nasty parasites that sucked and made a living from it, the political parties, power games, personal vendettas, the voracious pettiness of the frustrated: I want to be a general, I want to be rich [...] I want a boat, I want a house with a swimming pool, I want a technicolor TV set, I want a fancy lover [...] I want to screw over others, step on others, fuck others, I want to be alone, idolised and made of bronze, on a pedestal of staggering height'

As though to subscribe to Flaubert's memorable shorthand for his novelization of the 1848 revolution in *L'Éducation sentimentale*: "le sentimentalisme [...] suit la politique et en réproduit les phases" ["sentimentalism follows politics and reproduces its phases"], *Fado*'s parodically Dickensian plot is structured by a similar exchange of objects of desire. Hence, the private and the communications officer discover they have been in love with the same woman, the lieutenant-colonel's wife becomes the communications officer's lover, and the colonel's daughter turns out to be the lover of the second lieutenant's ex-wife. But, whereas in Flaubert, *style* emerges as the compensation for the baseness of the Real, in Antunes's novel, literary space offers no such consolation. It has itself become simulacral. It is not only that *Fado alexandrino* has reduced the most significant event in Portugal's recent history to a serial recapitulation of earlier models, a farce without even its tragic original, but its labyrinthine plot, the tropological exuberance of its descriptive language, the systematic imbrication of its narrative voices, and indeed its "alexandrine" structure itself, suggest an excessive diegetic control. They figure a modernist project which, like the Revolution, comes after the end of—and as a supplement to—a modernity which Portugal supposedly experienced only as an absence.

Fado alexandrino becomes, in this sense, the site of a temporal *post* to a *modo* that was always an empty place. In *Fado*, then, the revolutionary *no* [*não*] is never pressed into the service of a *yes*, as it is in Saramago's conventional dialectical reading of Portugal's recent history. It is canceled but not preserved. It remains *nothing*: an absence incessantly displaced and disguised as something else. Like the subject's desire for "that part of himself [that it] loses at birth," revolutionary desire, too, ultimately reveals its "essential affinity" with that "initial state from which the living entity has at one time or another departed and to which it is striving to return by the circuitous paths along which its development leads" (*Freud, Pleasure* 45), with "the zone of death," for "the [subject's] search [for] the part of himself lost forever [is] profoundly a death drive" (Lacan 198–9, 205).

In this way, the promise of new life which the April Revolution exemplifies in most of the war novels I examine above is radically refigured in Lobo Antunes' *Fado* as a familiar metropolitan death. Like Flaubert's *Sentimental Education*, *Fado alexandrino* closes with a "sacrifice" of sorts. In the last chapter, "the communications officer [lies] crucified on the carpet" (492), apparently as symbolic a figure as Dussardier in Flaubert's novel, who falls, "les bras en croix" ["his arms spread out as on a cross"] (446), cut down by his former friend and mentor Sénécal's saber on December 4, 1852, "the 18th Brumaire of Louis Bonaparte." Yet unlike Dussardier, Antunes's militant does not succumb with the name of the Republic on his lips. Indeed, echoing the claim of the protagonist of Manuel Alegre's *Jornada de África* that "tudo o que é acção e história e rasgo e risco se passa sempre do outro lado [...], nada acontece aqui" (19),[XXXIX] he consigns to History's proverbial dustbin his radical utopian dreams:

> Quem continua a preocupar-se com a revolução [...] quem persiste, neste país, em querer mudar o mundo, quando em Portugal, não é?, o mundo é que nos muda a nós [...] as pessoas alteram-se [...] mas as instituições nunca [...] terminam sempre [...] por regressar à tona, eternas, intactas, teimosas, invioladas, sempre [...] os mesmos ricos, os mesmos pobres. (Fado 504–5)[XL]

Occasioned by no identifiable motive or ideal (an accident, an obscure and senseless crime of passion?), the death of this former revolutionary is thus also supplementary, both too much and too late, yet another instance of narratorial and symbolic exuberance. An ironically fitting culmination to an abyssal utopian desire, it is as empty and exchangeable, as horrifically inconsequential as the meaningless sacrifices of Kafka's Joseph K. or Georg Bendemann. Ultimately, as all four veterans die in melodramatic succession at the end of the novel, the death of the communications officer is reinscribed in a chain of signifiers that mean always and ineluctably nothing. For Lobo Antunes, Portugal after the April Revolution, and in the wake of a series of risible attempts to contrive for itself a protagonist's role in the very same narrative of emancipation which it had evoked to legitimate its grisly colonial adventure, locates itself once again outside History. For "em Portugal [...] tudo estagna e se suspende no tempo" (*Ordem* 19).[XLI] In this light, the yearning for revolutionary salvation seems as deluded as the decrepit colonists' reverential waiting in *As naus* for King Sebastian's

XXXIX 'all that is action and history and tearing and risk happen elsewhere [...], nothing happens here'

XL 'Whoever remains thinking about the revolution [...] whoever hangs on, in this country, to wanting to change the world, when in Portugal, right?, the world rather changes us [...] people can change [...] but institutions never do [...] they always end up back to where they started, eternal, untouched, stubborn, unscathed, always [...] the same rich people, the same poor people'

XLI 'in Portugal [...] everything stops and drags in time'

foretokened ride across the ocean of time. And so it is that the Event that for almost half a century the whole nation had sedulously awaited at the edge of an historical void finally reveals itself in Antunes's *Fado* to be the very "História, com maiúscula ou com letra pequena, [que] já não passa por nós" (Alegre, *Jornada* 78).[XLII]

XLII 'History, with or without capital 'h,' [that] no longer flows through us'

In figuring the April Revolution as a foreclosure of History, Lobo Antunes's fiction reiterates its refusal to represent an "alternate" subjectivity. Whereas Alegre's and Melo's novels posit a third or "universal" moment in which an unpresentable and radically heterogenous enemy is ultimately reconciled with a reluctantly imperialist self, Antunes's *Fado* insists upon the incommensurability of metropolitan and (post)colonial times. Between the former and the latter a differend, the "heterogeneity of two distinct and discontinuous phrase regimens" (Lyotard 181), opens up. It is to this gap between the "truth" of the African struggles for independence and that of the process that led up to Portugal's April Revolution that Lobo Antunes attempts to pay heed in his writing. His narratives try in effect to track the waning currency of the West's notorious long narrative, to chronicle its reiterated failures to accomplish the enlightenment project of emancipation. They seek to inscribe in their interstices what Lyotard has called the liquidation of the project of modernity.

1 It is into a similar death wish that Oskar's "desire to return to the womb" (49) seems in effect to transform itself at his mother's funeral: "He wished to go down into the pit with Mama and the fetus. And there he wished to remain [...] until his mama for his sake and he for her sake should rot away" (165).

2 "The goal of centuries moving steadily toward tolerance, kindness, mutual understanding" (Carpentier 96).

3 Lourenço's title is obviously a tribute to Octavio Paz' imaginative psychoanalysis of Mexico's national character, *El labirinto de la soledad*.

4 "This space is not a delimiting line, but rather a fissure or fracture of a line; it is the 'threshold of capacity to which Conrad pointed though he never attained that capacity himself'" (López 46).

5 In my book *Imaginary Geographies in Portuguese and Lusophone-African Literature: Narratives of Discovery and Empire* (2007).

6 Published in English translation as *The Return of the Caravels*, this novel, the last of a quartet written after the "Angola trilogy," in a sense "literalizes" a metaphoric section of the quartet's third novel, *O Auto dos danados*, in which a character appears to hallucinate about boarding a train which lands him "em Lisboa perto de um rio enorme no qual navegavam caravelas e guindastes, no meio de descobridores de gibão, de barbas iluminadas por tormentas, especiarias e coqueiros, morrendo de escorbuto nos bancos da Avenida [...]. De tempos a tempos, à noite, uma furgoneta da polícia, recolhia travestis e vice-reis a caminho dos calabouços do Governo Civil, onde os funcionários [...] recebiam, surpreendidos, ameaças de enforcamento ou de degredo, gritadas por almirantes [...] num português medieval que encantava os homens-mulheres" (272–3). ["in Lisbon nearby a wide river where caravels and cranes sailed, amongst sailors in their gilets, and luscious beards lit by storms, spices and coconut trees, dying of scurvy on the benches of Avenida [...]. Every now and then at night, a police van would pick up crossdressers and gentlemen bringing them to the dungeons of the Central Hub, where clerks [...] were hurled death treats and profanities by the admirals [...] in a medieval Portuguese that delighted the she-males"].

7 The reading which follows significantly revises the one I offer in "The Discreet Seductiveness of the Crumbling Empire: Sex, Violence and Colonialism in the Fiction of António Lobo Antunes." In elaborating this revision, I have been especially indebted to Phyllis Peres's thoughtful critique of my position in "Love and Imagination among the Ruins of Empire: Antonio Lobo Antunes's *Os cus de Judas and Fado alexandrino*."

8 "The Negro / with the trumpet at his lips / Has dark moons of weariness beneath his eyes [...] The music from the trumpet at his lips is honey mixed with liquid fire" (Hughes 114).

Works Cited

Adorno, Theodor W. *Notes to Literature*. Vol. 1. Trans. Shierry Weber Nicholsen. Ed. Rolf Tiedemann. New York: Columbia UP, 1991. Print.

Alegre, Manuel and **Carlos Paredes**, "Explicação de Alcácer Quibir." *É preciso um país*. Lisbon: EMI / Valentim de Carvalho, 1974. Print.

Antunes, António Lobo. *A ordem natural das coisas*. Lisbon: Dom Quixote, 1992. Print.

—. *As naus*. Lisbon: Dom Quixote, 1988. Print.

—. *Auto dos danados*. Lisbon: Dom Quixote, 1990. Print.

—. *Fado alexandrino*. Lisbon: Dom Quixote, 1987. Print.

—. *Jornada de África*. Lisbon: Publicações Dom Quixote, 1989. Print.

—. *Os cus de Judas*. Lisbon: Dom Quixote, 1986. Print.

Baudelaire, Charles. *La Fanfarlo, Le Spleen de Paris: petits poèmes en prose*. Eds. David Scott and Barbara Wright. Paris: Flammarion, 1987. Print.

Carpentier, Alejo. *The Lost Steps*. Trans. Harriet de Onís. New York: Farrar, Straus and Giroux, 1989. Print.

Césaire, Aimé. *Collected Poetry*. Trans. and ed. Clayton Eshleman and Annette Smith. Berkeley: U of California P, 1983. Print.

Conrad, Joseph. *Heart of Darkness (with The Congo Diary)*. Ed. Robert Hampson. New York: Penguin Books, 1995. Print.

Flaubert, Gustave. *L'Éducation sentimentale*. Ed. S. de Sacy. Paris: Gallimard, 1965. Print.

Foucault, Michel. *Les mots et les choses: une archologie des sciences humaines*. Paris: Éditions Gallimard, 1966. Print.

—. *The Order of Things: An Archaeology of the Human Sciences*. Trans. Alan Sheridan. New York: Vintage Books, 1973. Print.

Freud, Sigmund. *Beyond the Pleasure Principle*. Trans. and ed. James Strachey. New York and London: W.W. Norton & Company, 1989. Print.

—. *Civilization and its Discontents*. Trans. and ed. James Strachey. New York: W. W. Norton & Company, 1989. Print.

—. "The Uncanny." Trans. Alix Strachey. *Psychological Writings and Letters*. Ed. Sander Gilman. New York: Continuum, 1995. Print.

Gilroy, Paul. *The Black Atlantic: Modernity and Double Consciousness*. Cambridge: Harvard UP, 1994. Print.

Grass, Günter. *Die Blechtrommel*. Frankfurt am Main: Lucterhand, 1974. Print.

Hegel, G.W. F. *The Philosophy of History*. Trans. J. Sibree. New York: Dover Publications, 1956. Print

—. *Philosophy of Mind* (together with the Zusatze). Trans. William Wallace and A.V. Miller. Oxford: Clarendon Press, 1971. Print.

Hughes, Langston. *Selected Poems of Langston Hughes*. New York: Vintage Books, 1974. Print.

James, C.L.R. *The C.L.R James Reader*. Ed. Anna Grimshaw. Oxford: Blackwell, 1992. Print.

Lacan, Jacques. *Four Fundamental Concepts of Psycho-Analysis*. Ed. Jacques-Alain Miller. Trans. Alan Sheridan. New York and London: W.W. Norton & Company, 1981. Print.

Lopez, Alfred J. *Posts and Pasts: A Theory of Postcolonialism*. Albany: SUNY Press, 2001. Print.

Lourenço, Eduardo. *O labirinto da saudade*. Lisbon: Dom Quixote: 1978. Print.

—. *Mitologia da saudade, seguido de Portugal como destino*. Sao Paulo: Companhia de Letras, 1999. Print.

Lyotard, Jean-François. *The Differend: Phrases in a Dispute*. Trans. Georges Van Den Abbele. Minneapolis: U of Minnesota P, 1988. Print.

Nietzsche, Friedrich. *The Birth of Tragedy (out of the Spirit of Music)*. Trans. Shaun Whiteside. Ed. Michael Tanner. New York: Penguin Books, 1993. Print.

Madureira, Luís. *Imaginary Geographies in Portuguese and Lusophone-African Literature: Narratives of Discovery and Empire*. New York: Mellen, 2007. Print.

—. "Tropical Sex Fantasies and the Ambassador's Other Death: The Difference in Portuguese Colonialism." *Cultural Critique* 28 (Fall 1994): 149-74. Print.

—. "The Discreet Seductiveness of the Crumbling Empire: Sex, Violence and Colonialism in the Fiction of António Lobo Antunes." *Luso-Brazilian Review* 32.1 (Summer 1995): 17–29. Print.

Peres, Phyllis. "Love and Imagination among the Ruins of Empire: Antonio Lobo Antunes's Os cus de Judas and Fado alexandrino." *After the Revolution: Twenty Years of Portuguese Literature*, 1974-1994. Eds. Helena Kaufman and Anna Klobucka. Lewisburg, PA and London, England: Bucknell UP; Associated UP, 1997. Print.

Said, Edward. *Culture and Imperialism*. New York: Vintage, 1993. Print.

Santos, Boaventura de Sousa. "11/92." *Luso-Brazilian Review* 29.1 (Summer 1992): 97-113.Print.

Saramago, José. *História do cerco de Lisboa*. Lisbon: Caminho, 1987. Print.

Sartre, Jean-Paul. *L'Existentialisme est un humanisme*. Paris: Nagel, 1970. Print.

Spivak, Gayatri Chakravorty. *A Critique of Postcolonial Reason: Toward a History of the Vanishing Present*. Cambridge: Harvard UP, 1999. Print.

—. Ed. and trans. *Imaginary Maps: Three Stories by Mahasweta Devi*. New York and London: Routledge, 1995. Print.

—. *Outside in the Teaching Machine*. New York and London: Routledge, 1993. Print.

NON FICTION

Autobiography Out of Empire

Lisa Lowe

in Chapter Two of *The Intimacies of Four Continents*, 43–71.
Duram, NC: Duke University Press, 2015.

In 1807, as Britain passed the Slave Trade Act to abolish the transatlantic African slave trade in the empire, Secretary of State Lord Hobart secretly dispatched Kenneth MacQueen to captain a ship named *Fortitude* from Bengal bound for Trinidad, carrying a cargo of Chinese workers and East India Company goods. When MacQueen's ship and the goods and people aboard were seized for a possible breach of laws relating to the Plantation Trade, there was an investigation, which later established that the voyage had been conducted under the Sanction of Her Majesty's Government. In other words, what surfaces in the historical record as the first British shipment of Chinese to the West Indies owes its appearance in the state archives to the ambiguous status of the voyage; the smuggled cargo was suspected of constituting a violation of the normative laws of maritime trade, suggesting the degree to which, in this period, the seas were an open, uncharted, and yet undetermined domain for mercantile expansion and imperial experiments beyond the nation-state.[1] In the late eighteenth century, as Britain sought to stabilize its place within a balance of power on the European continent, it also innovated new means to compete with transcolonial rivals France and Spain in the Americas, Asia, and the West Indies. From maps to travel narratives to literature like *Robinson Crusoe* or *Gulliver's Travels*, cultural representations of the transoceanic voyage mediated the imagined possibility and peril of a new *nomos* figured by the open seas.[2] The Chinese aboard the *Fortitude* shared the seas with Royal Navy men-o-war, mercantile trading ships, privateer ships, and vessels manned by merchant seamen, deserters, and escaped slaves.

Papers from MacQueen's hearing are collected and archived in the Colonial Office Correspondence at the National Archives in London. During the proceedings, the Solicitor-General G. L. Tuckett appealed MacQueen's case by stating British hopes that the "Trinidad experiment," to import Chinese "will eventually supercede the continuance of the Slave Trade in the West Indies."[3] Evidence presented in the MacQueen case to justify the smuggling of Chinese cargo included the 1803 "Secret Memorandum from the Colonial Office to the Chairman of the Board of Directors of the East India Company," in which administrators outlined the plan to import Chinese workers in order to resolve problems in the current system of slavery. Other documents included MacQueen's letter accepting the commission, in which MacQueen characterized the Chinese as "an industrious, sober, orderly people," and the statement by Attorney-General Archibald Gloster, who praised the plan to introduce Chinese into Trinidad by suggesting that, as a supplement to slave labor and the existing colonial social order, the Chinese would deter a possible insurrection of African slaves, and moreover, would form a racial "barrier" between the British and the "Negroes." In discussing the 1803 Memorandum in chapter 1, I suggested the instrumental use of the Chinese in the Colonial Office decision to employ liberal political discourse to reform a system of colonial labor that had been based on settler colonialism and slavery for over two centuries, and I observed that the representation of the Chinese as a "free race" belied the foreclosure of freedom and self-possession for the indigenous, the enslaved, and the indentured alike.

In this chapter, I turn to examine the form, genre, and significance of the eighteenth-century narrative of freedom overcoming slavery, even and especially when promised freedoms were not borne out in practice. The Colonial Office description of the Chinese as "free" suggests first that this abstract notion of "freedom" not only denied the coercion through which Chinese laborers were brought to the Americas, but it also masked the ongoing settler appropriation and slavery that were the conditions for the colonial plantations into which the Chinese were brought. Furthermore, the representation of the Chinese as "free" suggests the degree to which promised freedoms—both as political rights and free wage labor—were crucial concepts not only in the discussion of the abolition and emancipation in the colonies, but were significant to the management and discipline of laborers in England, as well. At the turn of the nineteenth century, definitions of free wage labor in England were deeply implicated in debates about the abolition of slavery in the West Indian and North American colonies. In his study of the end of the transatlantic slave trade, historian David Eltis observes that despite the large gap between the two labor systems—enslaved African labor in the colonies and wage labor in England—abolition was a central piece of a utilitarian experiment in social engineering being conducted in both locations.[4]

The liberal reformers, who addressed conditions for wage labor in England by introducing legislation concerning a ten-hour day and restrictions on child labor, were among the same groups who advocated for the Slave Trade Act of 1807 and the Slavery Abolition Act of 1833. English Whigs argued that the termination of the slave trade and the abolition of slavery would lead to a "free wage" relationship between master and slave, and saw the end of slavery as necessary to the implementation of liberal utilitarian laissez-faire principles of the work ethic, industry, civilization, and greater productivity in England. Jeremy Bentham, James Mill, and John Stuart Mill at the *Westminster Review* argued that free trade and a free market economy were necessary solvents both to destroy paternalistic controls, and to overcome the remnants of slavery.[5] Paradoxically, the liberal arguments to end slavery contributed to the ideology of free wage labor that was necessary to buttress industrialization at home, even while coerced labor remained highly profitable in the colonies. The proposal of Chinese, and soon after Indian, indentured labor in the colonies presented an intermediary "solution" to this dilemma. While antislavery ideas prevailed in Britain, indentured labor in the colonies could be represented as part of a system of free labor that appeared commensurate with ideas of free labor at home.

One aim of this book is to understand the role of liberal freedoms of wages, rights, and trade, and their literary and cultural forms in Europe and North America, within the broader historical context of colonial labor and production that linked transatlantic African slavery and Asian in-denture in the Americas and throughout the emerging Anglo-American empire. Many social and economic historians have characterized this period as the "transition from slavery to free labor." The very notion of "transition" conveys the sense of progressive development from one stage to another, implying that the system of slavery was gradually superseded by a new system of free wage labor, and by the granting of political enfranchisement.[6] I am arguing, to the contrary, for a quite different understanding of the relationship between "slavery" and "freedom." Rather than presuming a linear understanding of historical progress, in which the slavery of the past was overcome and replaced by modern freedoms, I emphasize instead that in the late eighteenth and early nineteenth centuries the narrative of freedom overcoming slavery was canonized in British and European political and economic spheres, in discourses of citizenship, free labor, and free trade. The desire for promised freedoms came to discipline and organize varieties of social subjects, those enfranchised and those not or never to be, working in conditions of coercion and exploitation, in Europe and North America, and throughout the colonized world. As Britain moved from mercantilist plantation production toward command of an expanded international trade in manufactured goods, the Chinese indentured worker appears in British colonial and parliamentary papers as a figure for this emerging "transition" to "freedom," referring to a modern mode of administering and dividing laboring groups through the liberal promise of freedom that would commence with the end of slavery. In this chapter and the next, I inquire into the relationship between liberalism and colonialism by suggesting that literary and cultural *genres* emerged alongside liberal economics and political philosophy, and that autobiography and the novel did some of the important work of mediating and resolving liberalism's contradictions.

Commensurate with political philosophy's affirmation of the individual's passage to freedom through economic industry and political emancipation, the *autobiography* served as a particularly powerful genre for the individual achievement of liberty through ethical education and civilization. In a sense, the autobiography is the liberal genre par excellence. It is the modern narrative expression of the individual subject providing evidence of not only the imperatives and privileges of liberal subjects, but also its aesthetic form. Attention to the autobiography's form, as well as to narrative contradictions and contesting voices, suggests methods for reading the subjugated histories that inhabit the narratives of individual rights and democratic freedoms. Considering Equiano's *Interesting Narrative of the Life of Olaudah Equiano*, or *Gustavus Vassa, the African, Written by Himself* (1789), in relation to various literary conventions, and other paradigmatic narratives, such as Ottobah Cugoano's *Thoughts and Sentiments on the Evil and Wicked Traffic of the Slavery and Commerce of the Human Species* (1787) or the *Autobiography of Benjamin Franklin* (1793), both illuminates features of this liberal genre and calls attention to the tensions and inconsistencies that arise when the genre of liberty shapes the story of a former slave.

The *Interesting Narrative* states that Equiano was born in Essaka, a province of Eboe in the West African kingdom of Benin in 1745, and it recounts his capture into slavery as a young boy, being separated from his kin, and moved from slave ship to plantation, from master to master. Acquiring the skills of sailing a ship, learning to write, measure, and do arithmetic, Equiano serves in battles, works commercial ships, and gradually earns and saves enough to purchase his own freedom. He recounts formerly having been cargo in the Atlantic market in people, and how he came to participate in the transatlantic commerce within which he and others like him had been mere property.[7] As a literate Christian man, he abhors the brutality of West Indian slavery in the words of Milton's *Paradise Lost* and savors his freedom with allusions to the books of Acts, Kings, and Exodus from the Old Testament. Equiano's accomplishment of freedom refers allegorically to Dante's journeys, the trials of Jesus, the travels of Gulliver, and the adventures of Robinson Crusoe. In addition to these allusions, the autobiographer marks his humanity sentimentally in expressions of interiority and feeling, legally by his papers of manumission, and economically by his industry as a merchant marine, after which the sea that was once the traumatic site across which he was cruelly taken becomes the body he now commands. He seeks appointment as an Anglican missionary with the Sierra Leone Resettlement and favors the development of commerce and trade between Europe and Africa. In 1792, the author proudly added to later editions of *The Interesting Narrative* that Equiano married and had two daughters. In this sense, Equiano's self-narration circumnavigates from Africa to the Americas to England as the tale moves from Eboe childhood to modern commercial bourgeois man and father. As Houston Baker Jr. observed, Equiano "masters the rudiments of economics that condition his very life."[8] Yet even as Equiano's text has been taken to epitomize the most eloquent narration of individual redemption through modern liberal institutions, upholding the theological, political, and economic arguments made by British abolitionists, like later slave narratives from *The History of Mary Prince* (1831) to *The Narrative of the Life of Frederick Douglass* (1845), Equiano's *Interesting Narrative* contains important digressions and interruptions that mark the limits of the genre for containing and resolving the contradictions of colonial slavery.

Equiano's passage to liberty expressed the "structure of feeling" of what scholars have termed the "Atlantic world" or "global eighteenth century," encompassing the height of the transatlantic slave trade, antislavery movements, formal abolition of the trade, and the collective upheavals expressed in revolutions in France, the United States, and Saint-Domingue.[9] Like Kenneth MacQueen, the captain charged by the British Colonial Office and East India Company to import Chinese workers, Equiano was also a seaman, more at home on a ship than settled in a particular nation. His narrative of liberty gained through Atlantic crossing is similar to what Laura Doyle observes of the "Atlantic novel," a tradition of Anglo-Atlantic and African Atlantic writing in which a "liberty plot" crosses the Atlantic Ocean to enact a dialectic of freedom and empire. While MacQueen and Equiano could be considered members of the "new world Atlantic" working class made up of sailors, slaves, and commoners elaborated by Peter Linebaugh and Marcus Rediker's *Many-Headed Hydra*, the autobiography made evident that even as a freed man, Equiano's relationship to transatlantic commerce would be haunted by his former enslavement. As Cathy Davidson aptly observes, Equiano's autobiography portrayed "a man who is free enough to sail virtually all the seven seas yet who ever remains one step away from recapture and return into slavery."[10] His narrative stylized the so-called transition from slavery to freedom and dramatized a conversion from chattel to liberal subject that at once negotiated the voices of abolition and slave resistance, and mediated the logics of coloniality in which trade in people and goods connected Africa, plantation Virginia, the colonial West Indies, and metropolitan England. It exemplified a fluency in the languages for defining and delimiting humanity, from liberal political philosophy and Christian theology, to the mathematical reason necessary for economy, trade, and navigation. Yet the achievement of Equiano's "freedom" was ever tenuous; kidnapped, traded, and captured, he is transferred from one owner to another; once his manumission is purchased, his life as a freed man is continuously threatened by the possibility of forcible abduction and reenslavement.

The historical man named Olaudah Equiano appears in parliamentary records as an important figure in the British abolition movement, and his autobiography was also a central artifact in the efforts to end the slave trade. The *Interesting Narrative* gained the attention of Equiano's contemporaries, the abolitionists William Wilberforce, Granville Sharp, John Wesley, and Thomas Clarkson, who opposed slavery as an immoral, corrupting influence on English and Africans alike; as Christians, they were anxious to demonstrate that Africans were members of the brotherhood of man under God, with human qualities that made them deserving of freedom. Wilberforce, in his 1789 speech on the Abolition of the Slave Trade, spoke of the transit of slaves to the West Indies: "This, I confess, in my opinion is the most wretched part of the whole subject. *So much misery condensed in so little room*, is more than the human imagination had ever before conceived.... Let anyone imagine to himself, 6 or 700 of these wretches chained two and two, surrounded with every object that is nauseous and disgusting, diseased, and struggling under every kind of wretchedness!—How can we bear to think of such a scene as this?"[11] As if the rejoinder to his appeal to imagine the inconceivable, Wilberforce presented Equiano's *Interesting Narrative* along with petitions to end the slave trade to Parliament. Wilberforce praised it not only as a treatise against the slave trade, but for its eloquence as an autobiography written by an African with memories of a West African childhood, the Middle Passage, and the tortures and abuses of slaves in the West Indies, whose education, religion, and exceptional determination culminated in earned freedom.[12] Generations of critics since then have heralded the autobiography as *the* singular narrative demonstrating the overcoming of slavery and fitness for freedom.

The canonization of Equiano's text as the first autobiography in English by an enslaved African produces a structural paradox in which its elevation as a paradigm for liberal freedom has often involved the burial of the more complex currents of the transatlantic world on which that freedom rests. The intense social value accorded the autobiographical genre illustrates how liberal emancipation required a literary narrative of the self-authoring autonomous individual to be distilled out of the heteronomous collective subjectivity of colonial slavery. This is as much a literary critical question of how the autobiography is interpreted—whether we read it as a fluid story of a unitary author's successful development of reason, sentiment, industry, and freedom, or whether we read for the ellipses, interruptions, contradictory shifts in voice or tempo that surround particular episodes—as it is a historiographical matter of which archives, events, temporalities and geographies will be privileged in the situating of Equiano's story. Moreover, it asks us to consider how liberalism requires mediation through an aesthetic form that encourages readers to understand the emancipation of the individual *as if it were* a collective emancipation. As the autobiographical subject writes his life, and comes to possess the meaning of slavery as his own "past," the genre does the work of subjugating the history of the collective enslaved within a regulative temporality in which slavery is only legible as a distant origin out of which the free modern subject can emerge. As such, autobiography, a genre of liberal political narrative that affirms individual right, may precisely contribute to the "forgetting" of the collective subject of colonial slavery, a heteronomous subaltern collectivity necessary to colonial slavery and its abolition. When abolitionists like Wilberforce promoted Equiano's tale of individual liberty as the representative slave narrative, the exemplary qualities selected to illustrate the humanity of the slave may have subsumed the persistence of slavery, for those still in bondage at the time of the autobiography, as well as for those who would be "emancipated" in the aftermath. The exemplary tale of individual freedom had the power to defer the larger scale transformation of slavery as a collective condition in the empire.

Inasmuch as a comparison between MacQueen and Equiano underscores the distinction between the seafaring captain and the seaman who had been property, so too does drawing a contrast between Equiano's autobiography and, for example, that of his transatlantic contemporary, Benjamin Franklin. The contrast reveals the limits to the former slave's access to writing, print, and the public sphere of politics in England and the United States. Franklin's autobiography is widely heralded as a portrait of the life of the philosopher-statesman as representative of the moral qualities of the new American nation; the *bildung* of Franklin's development from self-educated youth to civic maturity expressed an emerging American exceptionalism, the notion that the new nation, founded on democratic egalitarian principles, was different than that of older European empires. Like Equiano's, Franklin's exceptional life emerged out of transatlantic conditions; the first two parts of Franklin's *Autobiography* were written in Europe, the first in England in 1771, the second in France in 1784. The narrative of the singular man embodied the values of hard work, moderation, sobriety, self-improvement, and civic responsibility, as he participated in the rebellion of the American colonies, the Constitutional Convention, and the writing of the Declaration of Independence. Franklin was a printer by trade, a dedicated public servant who founded libraries and utilities and made contributions to science; his printing mediated the formation of the public sphere in the early republic, and scholars note how Franklin used the medium of letters and print culture to frame his individual life as a representation of American national destiny.[13] Franklin's *Autobiography* made evident many of the formal features that later established the autobiography as the predominant genre for narration of the liberal life: the accomplishment of exemplary freedom of person and nation through industry, moral regeneration, and civic duty. Yet while Equiano's autobiography also exemplified reason, probity, humility, and thrift, the narrative of the self-taught former slave is marked, again and again, by the limits to his attainment of freedom.

The *Interesting Narrative* drew from and contributed to various literary traditions, forms of knowledge, and social discourses, which illuminate its significance, as well. Equiano's autobiography took up the "noble savage" trope established in Aphra Behn's *Oroonoko* (1688), which thematized Britain's "new world" colonial encounters in the figure of the African prince; it exemplified the sentimentalism that characterized later British Romantic representations of slavery, from Robert Burns's *The Slave's Lament* to William Blake's *Little Black Boy* and William Cowper's *The Negro's Complaint*; and it was a Black Atlantic forerunner of the African American slave narrative. In Behn's heroic romance, Oroonoko, the grandson of an African king, falls in love with Imoinda, and their love is thwarted when both are sold into slavery, until the two lovers are reunited in Surinam. Oroonoko organizes a slave revolt, which is defeated by military forces led by an English deputy who also desires Imoinda. To protect Imoinda from violation by enemies after his death, the two lovers plan that Oroonoko should take her life first. Mourning Imoinda, Oroonoko is captured and executed by gruesome public dismemberment. Oroonoko is a romantic hero suffering with grace in love and battle, governed by a code of honor. From the narrator's opening description, we see the logic of coloniality at work: the figuration of Oroonoko as a "royal African" acknowledges colonial slavery by granting the exemplary African a nobility that is conveyed through the comparison to the European aristocracy: "His Nose was rising and *Roman*, instead of *African* and flat," and "he had nothing of Barbarity in his Nature, but in all Points address'd himself, as if his Education had been in some *European* Court."[14]

The "royal slave" is not merely a displacement of the unrepresentable trade in African slaves, but the figure condenses a variety of global practices. Chi-ming Yang, for example, suggests that the figure of Oroonoko romanticizes the African slave trade through a particular form of commodification, that of early modern orientalism; that is, both Imoinda's "japanned" skin and Oroonoko's "Polished Jet" blackness of "statuary" proportions render them aestheticized as if they are lacquer figures, ornamental chinoiserie, referencing the porcelains, silk embroideries, and wallpapers that were part of the already burgeoning Asian trades.[15] Srivinas Aravamudan invents the term *oroonokoism* to capture this particular orientalist domestication of the African prince as "pet"; the exceptional prince simultaneously represents and occludes the violent historical conditions of colonial encounters.[16] The English female narrator's sympathy for the suffering African prince sentimentalizes colonial slavery and trade, even as it habituates the metropolitan English community to it. Oroonoko's honorable feeling "humanizes" him, as the narrator and reader are likewise humanized by their benevolent and sentimental identification with him. The narrative first models and then manages the tenderness that Oroonoko himself will display as he mourns his beloved, recalling Adam Smith's formulation that "moral sentiment" is that we "place ourselves in his situation, we conceive ourselves enduring all the same torments, we enter as it were into his body, and become in some measure the same person with him."[17] The trope of the "royal slave" unjustly chained, and ultimately destroyed for leading the rebellion that is the inevitable consequence of slavery, opens the way for Equiano's *Interesting Narrative*, as well as for the eighteenth-century sentimental tradition that became a staple of Anglophone antislavery narratives and liberal republicanism in Britain and the United States for the next century and a half.[18] Equiano's autobiography mastered and deftly employed these sentimental rhetorics that pleaded for the slave's humanity by giving voice to the enslaved and that aimed at stirring the reader into action. Yet however much sentimentalism gave voice to the slave's suffering and instructed the English reader to sympathize, sentimental identification did not innocently humanize or civilize the slave, as it often reworked the violence of slavery as a resource for the reading public's moral position.[19] If sentimentalism defines humanity through emotion and governs its transfer from the feeling human subject to the abject thing, this is nowhere clearer than in Thomas Bicknell and John Day's 1773 poem, *The Dying Negro*, well known and famously celebrated by British abolitionists.[20] Bicknell and Day's inspiration for the poem was a newspaper account of an African slave who, upon being returned to the ship from which he had fled to marry a white fellow servant, killed himself rather than be captured and returned to slavery in the West Indies. Like other abolitionist poems that "gave voice" to the slave's lament, *The Dying Negro* expresses the anguish of the man who sought death rather than be condemned to it by slave masters. Through poems such as this, abolitionists aimed to inspire the pity of the responsive reader, to engage them in the antislavery cause. Yet as the sentimental poem converted the violent conditions of slavery into occasions for English benevolence, it performed what Lynn Festa calls an act of "affective piracy" in which the liberal poet made sentimental value of the other's plight.[21]

In Equiano's *Interesting Narrative*, the use of sentimentalism is rendered more complex through the generic conceit in which the narrator tells the story of his life as if it is unfolding, balancing the perspectives of the slave he was, with that of the literate freed man he has become. Thus, the moment that the autobiographer cites at length a full stanza of Bicknell and Day's poem *The Dying Negro* is significant, for it emphasizes the cleaving of the narrative subject, and it marks the point at which the free author portrays his former self and others as abject slaves. In the first four chapters, the autobiography recounts the plight of Equiano as a young boy, abducted, traded, and enslaved. When he is brought to the first slave ship, he represents his understanding of slavery through a process in which he sees himself in the enslaved condition of the "multitude": "[As I saw] a multitude of black people of every description chained together, every one of their countenances expressing dejection and sorrow, I no longer doubted of my fate."[22] He is transported from Africa to the West Indies to England and back to the West Indies again; he received various names, including "Gustavus Vassa" from a captain aboard one of the many ships. In chapter 5, when the young narrator believes himself to be on the threshold of manumission, he is suddenly seized, sold again, and returned to slavery in the West Indies, which he describes as being "plunged...in a new slavery," with miseries that are "tenfold" what he knew earlier (70). He recounts young Vassa's horror at witnessing the cruel rape of female slaves and children, men staked to the ground, mutilated, burned, caged, branded, hung, muzzled, and flogged, all of which not only indicate the cruel inhumanity of the slave system, but also emphasize that the young slave was unaware then of what the adult author would realize later, that "slavery" was, in a metaphorical sense, a state of unknowing to be overcome by the power to know oneself, expressed in self-authorship. The narratologist Gerard Genette famously elaborated the trope of *metalepsis* to discuss the moments in a narrative when there is an interruption of one time by another, when there is a transgression of boundaries between "the world *in* which one tells and the world *of* which one tells."[23] Throughout Equiano's autobiography, the separation of these two levels remains mostly invisible, and the diegetic narrative largely subsumes the former in order to showcase the latter. Yet when the narrative breaks off and the autobiographer cites Bicknell and Day's poem, the perspectives of the later freed man and the slave he once was are foregrounded and emphasized. The narrator evokes his former feelings as a young slave through the words of the poem's "dying Negro," who calls on death to relieve him from horror and dread of recapture, punishment, and enslavement. He asks that he might be in that place:

> Where slaves are free, and men oppress no more.
> Fool that I was, inur'd so long to pain,
> To trust to hope, or dream of joy again.
> Now *dragg'd* once more beyond the western main,
> To groan beneath some dastard planter's *chain*;
> Where my poor countrymen in *bondage* wait
> The long enfranchisement of ling'ring *fate*:
> Hard ling'ring *fate*!
> While, ere the dawn of day,
> Rous'd by the *lash* they go their cheerless way;
> And as their souls with *shame* and anguish burn,
> Salute with groans *unwelcome morn*'s return,
> And, *chiding* ev'ry hour the slow-pac'd sun,

Pursue their *toils* till all his race is run.
No eye to mark their *suff'rings* with a tear;
No friend to comfort, and *no hope* to cheer:
Then, like the dull unpity'd brutes, a repair
To stalls as wretched, and as coarse a fare;
Thank heaven one day of mis'ry was o'er,
Then sink to sleep, and wish to wake no more.
(73, emphasis mine)

To convey the relief that death would bring to the slave, each line of the verse names a form of bondage—from "chains" and "fate" to "lash" and "toil"—to enlist the readers' pity for the "Negro" forcibly kept enslaved. But the autobiographical narrator's citation of the poem also dramatizes the very operations through which subject cleaves from object, through which the perspective of the individual "Negro" is educed out of the collective subject of "my poor countrymen" and "dull unpity'd brutes." This process that differentiates the autobiographer from the collective enslaved is repeated in Equiano's performance of his initial identification with, and then distinction from, the "multitude," and then again, in his disappearance into the "voice" of Bicknell and Day. The extensive citation not only makes evident how well "Equiano" understood sentimental literature as the vehicle for establishing sympathy as the sign of the human, and its centrality to moral arguments against slavery, but in "giving voice" to the young slave's suffering in the words of Bicknell and Day, the autobiography permits "Equiano," *and* the "multitude," to be "spoken for" by the English abolitionists. At the same time, by enlisting sentimental identification to bestow a voice and consciousness to the young slave he was, the autobiographer paradoxically inhabits and displaces the position occupied by Bicknell and Day. As *The Interesting Narrative* performs literary sentimentalism to define free humanity over against the abject slaves, it precisely cites the sentimental poem as *the* literary convention established for this operation, and in the process foregrounds Equiano's difference as formerly racialized property, implying the "limits" of manumitted "freedom," and the impossibility that the former slave could ever *be* Bicknell and Day.

The Interesting Narrative also contributed to a large, diverse body of literature and knowledge attesting to the inhumanity of slavery from the perspective of African slaves. In alluding to other Black Atlantic narratives such as *The Life of James Albert Ukawsaw Gronnosiosaw, an African Prince, as Related by Himself* (1770), the *Narrative of the Lord's Wonderful Dealings with John Marrant, A Black* (1785), and fellow ex-slave Ottobah Cugoano's *Thoughts and Sentiments on the Evil and Wicked Traffic of the Slavery and Commerce of the Human Species* (1787), it provided first-person narrative descriptions of the conditions of slavery and attested to the proximity of freed Blacks to recapture and return to enslavement.[24] These Black Atlantic accounts not only represented the terrors of captivity and the enslaved man's resolve to be free, but they recorded travel across land and sea and were also informal botanical, oceanographic, and anthropological resources on nature, custom, and terrain of the African Gold Coast, the West Indies, England, and North America, which constituted a vernacular knowledge counter to the colonial taxonomies of Linnaeus and others, whose natural history served as a parallel discourse of colonial domestication.[25]

Cugoano's 1787 *Thoughts and Sentiments* was a richly polemical argument against the slave trade, which recorded his kidnapping, captivity on the slave ship, slavery itself, and experiences in England.[26] Unlike *The Interesting Narrative*, however, Cugoano's text does not present his life as a developmental ascent from slavery to freedom but emphasizes that he was "brought from a state of innocence and freedom, and, in a barbarous and cruel manner, conveyed to a state of horror and slavery" and maintains that "the extreme bitterness of grief and woe, that no language can describe" remains "though my fears and tears have long since subsided"(95). If Equiano's *Interesting Narrative* fluently recites the narrative of freedom overcoming slavery, one of the means through which the text attests to the unremediated condition of slavery is through its references to and resonances with Cugoano's more polemical, and less compromising, antislavery text. Equiano's descriptions of the capture and treatment of slaves often echo those of his contemporary Cugoano. Together, with other Black Atlantic writers, their works constituted and shaped a virtual inventory of the tropes, patterns of expression, and references whose recitation came to authorize later slave narratives.[27] Not only did they establish stories of brutal captivity, the transatlantic crossing, and religious conversion and deliverance, and invert the associations of white civilization and black barbarism; they also made recognizable to diverse publics the cruel commonplaces of slavery. Equiano's descriptions of the "multitude of black people of every description chained together, every one of their countenances expressing dejection and sorrow" (Equiano, 39) recall Cugoano's "rattling of chains, smacking of whips, and the groans and cries of our fellow-men" (Cugoano, 9). The repeated mention of "chains," whips," "groans," and "cries" works like a haunting and horrifying refrain, with immediately recognizable references to the body of knowledge about slavery. Moreover, both Equiano and Cugoano allude repeatedly to the slave's appeal to death as a release from the horrendous captivity of enslavement. Yet Cugoano's repeated use of "we" conveys his identification with the collective enslaved for whom "death was more preferable than life" (Cugoano, 10), while Equiano's narrative more often assumes the sentimental attitude of the abolitionist, and rhetorically individualizes himself while contemplating the suffering of slaves as a "multitude" or as "poor creatures": "Is it surprising that usage like this should drive the poor creatures to despair, and make them seek a refuge in death from those evils which render their lives intolerable" (Equiano, 80).

Difference of genre provides a clear way to distinguish the two narratives. As autobiography, *The Interesting Narrative* exemplifies the liberal imperative that the "life" emplot the transition from slavery to freedom, and in this way, it attests to the power of political emancipation, and Christian redemption. Cugoano's *Thoughts and Sentiments* was not an autobiography, but a treatise against slavery, and thus did not conform to this imperative; in a perpetual present tense, it testifies instead to the persistent human anguish of the enslaved in the face of slavery's excesses and the systemic dehumanization of the slaves. Cugoano represents his emancipation, literacy, and conversion to Christianity, not as deliverance, but as circumstances that permit the deepening of his struggles against slavery; the "groans and cries of the murdered" (58) continue unabated within Cugoano's text. In this sense, when Equiano's autobiography echoes Cugoano's account, it evokes this longer, unremediated collective condition of inhuman cruelty and survival. British abolitionists read Equiano's *Interesting Narrative* as a life that fulfilled Christian redemption and liberal economy. Yet slaves, ex-slaves, and others could "listen" to the complex tones of Equiano's narrative, and hear the "otherness" embedded within the text. They might recognize the allusions to death as deliverance from slavery, the double voicing one hears if listening to the lower frequencies, what Fred Moten calls the "freedom drive" dissonant to commodification and objectification, heard beneath and through a dominant genre.[28] Likewise, inasmuch as the "freedom" of the second half of the autobiography may work to redeem the "enslavement" of the first half, the narrative form cannot overcome the most profound offenses with which *The Interesting Narrative* begins: the slave traders' indifference to the sufferings of men, women, and children captured and chained, the terror and claustrophobia of the Middle Passage, the inhuman trade in human beings. Although *The Interesting Narrative* formally declares the conditions of slavery transcended by his individual liberty, their residues remain after the formal translation of colonial slavery into the conventions of the liberal autobiographical genre.

Perhaps equally important, Equiano has held a significant place in African American letters, and in the slave narrative tradition that followed him, heralded as a forerunner of the nineteenth-century African American slave narratives of Frederick Douglass, Harriet Jacobs, and others.[29] *The Interesting Narrative* exemplified crucial features of the antebellum slave narratives, which, as Frances Smith Foster has observed, drew on the Judeo-Christian structure of mortification, conversion, struggle, and jubilation; the captivity narrative; and the spiritual autobiography; as well as the rhetorics of liberalism.[30] Henry Louis Gates Jr. famously identified the powerful trope of the "Talking Book" in Equiano's eighteenth-century slave narrative, and the thematic importance of literacy to Black humanity.[31] The contradictions of Equiano's split voice—at one moment speaking as part of an enslaved collectivity, at another as the individual apart—can be explained in terms of the conditions for Black autobiography discussed by William Andrews: "From the outset of black autobiography in America, the presupposition reign[ed] that a black narrator needs a white reader to complete his text, to build a hierarchy of abstract significance on the mere matter of his facts, to supply a presence where there was only 'Negro,' only a dark absence."[32] Robert Stepto discussed this as a conflict between the slave's "tale" and the white abolitionists' "guarantee," which John Sekora called the "black message" in the "white envelope."[33] Critics have found in the aesthetic density of the antebellum slave narrative voices vying for control of different meanings and readerships.[34] Whether they have termed these rhetorical strategies "signifying," "riffing," "improvising," or "mo'nin,' " scholars of Black aesthetics have identified strategies that recode, double, and turn dominant meanings through indirection, parody, allusion, and association.[35]

Hazel Carby urges us to read Equiano's *Interesting Narrative* as neither strictly African nor European, but as a "new transatlantic Black autobiographical tradition," expressing the "geopolitics of encounter."[36] In a similar manner, Srinivas Aravamudan reads the autobiography as multiple, complex voices alternately jostling for characterization and narrativization as "Christian," "African," and "literate," while Christine Levecq observes Equiano's "unique black internationalism" that moves through "multiple anchorings."[37] In this sense, while Equiano's *Interesting Narrative* established the genre of autobiography for the Black subject's passage from slavery to freedom, his text has always been profoundly complex and contradictory; alternately voiced as slave narrative, seafaring tale, protoanthropology, sentimental literature, religious conversion, and abolitionist treatise, it is a hybrid, multivocal collaboration that enlisted and mediated the contradictions of the age to create its first-person autobiographical narrative.[38] Some readings celebrate Equiano's triumph over slavery, while others condemn its assimilation of commercial and colonial projects.[39] Carby writes: "Equiano speaks as a composite subject, a subject inhabiting multiple differences, as African, as black, as British, as Christian, as a diasporic and transnational citizen of the world, and in the process offers his readers the possibility of imagining a more complex cultural and national identity for themselves."[40] Aravamudan discusses Equiano as undergoing a "tropical baptism by English literary history and emerging as a sailor and a writer."[41]

Narrative temporality is itself a powerful vehicle of liberal progress, as evidenced in the emplotment of slave emancipation, in which the slave subject develops in time, constituting a story of an enslaved past that culminates in freedom achieved in the present. Just as we might read the multivocality of Equiano's *Interesting Narrative* as an interruption of the singular voice required by the autobiographical genre, its uses of temporal digression also destabilize the generic conventions of linear progressive development. Recent scholars have criticized the singular, secular temporality often employed in histories of slavery that subordinate many contending and converging "times"; they counter that the slave trade and slavery constituted other ways of "being in time." Historian Walter Johnson, for example, notes that the slaves' journeys began in the interior of Africa, and thus that a "First Passage" before the treacherous crossing of the "Middle Passage" is obscured by the narrative histories that presume the history of slavery begins with the European slave traders' encounter with Africa. In contrast, Equiano's autobiography layers and intertwines a constellation of "times": from the Christian time of an afterlife of eternity, to the African time of past and present events rather than strict sequence directed toward a future.[42] In her history of the conversion of captive people into commodities, Stephanie Smallwood juxtaposes the time of the slave trader, registered in ship's logs that marked time in terms of weather, disease, and slave mortality, with the time of men, women, and children chained in the holds of ships, seized by the "saltwater horror" of the Middle Passage, an "experience of motion without discernible direction or destination."[43] Saidiya Hartman conceives the "time of slavery" as a continuous relation between the past and the present, in which the present is *still* the "time of slavery," an aftermath in which slavery has not ended, but infuses the conditions, memories, and possibilities of the present.[44] This conception of the "time of slavery," in which "then and now coexist," negates the idea of "progress" and stresses the irreparable and unredeemable nature of the event of slavery; it insists that the liberal remedy of emancipation has not resolved the injustices of slavery and its subsequent inequalities. Hartman writes: "For the distinction between the past and the present founders on the interminable grief engendered by slavery and its aftermath. How might we understand mourning, when the event has yet to end?" Hartman's concept of the "time of slavery" belies the liberal narrative of development in time and asserts that emancipation from the violence of captivity, loss of homeland, expropriation of labor, and obliteration of kin and family has not yet occurred, is still yet to come.[45]

There are several key moments from the autobiography that dramatize colonial slavery as the limit to the promises of liberal economy, political emancipation, and Christian redemption. Though Equiano condemned slavery as inhuman commerce, he asserted that British civilization and laws of economic exchange would benefit Africans. Through these laws, Equiano sold his labor for a wage, permitting him to accumulate enough money to purchase and own himself. In describing his "disgust" at the West Indies, Equiano named as barbaric not only the inhuman torture of slaves, but the mode of production itself: a slavery system in which unwaged labor is forcibly stolen through terror and punishment. Over and over again, *The Interesting Narrative* exposed the historically specific relationship between racial slavery and capitalism, and yet Equiano's story suggests that he might achieve political freedom through the mastery of that economy: Equiano claimed his individual productivity out of the barbarism of unwaged slavery, proposing in a Lockean manner to sell the fruits of his "free labor" to become Smith's economic man. Vincent Carretta notes that Equiano, in a sense, commodified himself through his successful narrative autobiography; he retained copyright and kept most of the profits of the nine editions published between 1789 and 1974, earning an amount of British sterling equivalent to $120,000.[46] The Black autobiographer mastered the seas, the liberal public, and the symbolic economy of colonial slavery. The autobiography ends with an affirmation of the importance of expanding free enterprise and commerce between Britain and Africa. Yet inasmuch as the *Narrative* conforms to the autobiography of the liberal political economic subject, we can also see Equiano's journey as one of continual transgressions—across boundaries of nation, of property and subject, land and sea. As David Kazanjian observes, Equiano's movements cross the "ambiguously national space of the Atlantic" and reach "racial-national limits" that open up contradictions that cannot be contained by the liberal formalism of the autobiography.[47]

Three particular moments in Equiano's *Interesting Narrative* stand out as instances in which the autobiography foregrounds the tensions and contradictions of liberal emancipation. One occurs shortly after his manumission, when Equiano finds himself aboard a ship with a new captain boasting of his skill by steering a dangerous new course. In the middle of the night, stormy seas cause the ship to crash against rocks, and the captain immediately orders the hatches to be nailed down on the twenty slaves in the hold, sacrificing the slaves to save the Englishmen who will fit in the small escape boat. Equiano writes of realizing that the captain's calculus valued English lives over those of African slaves: it "rushed upon my mind that instant with such violence, that it quite overpowered me. . . . I could no longer restrain my emotion, and I told him he deserved drowning for not knowing how to navigate the vessel" (113). Equiano works quickly with the "black and creole" sailors on board to save the ship, defying the rational economic logic that privileged wage labor as individual property that he had otherwise promoted. Equiano's accession to bourgeois manhood takes the form of becoming a merchant marine, a seaman much like Kenneth MacQueen, the smuggler of Chinese "coolies" commissioned in the 1803 "Secret Memorandum" discussed earlier. Like Kenneth MacQueen, Equiano becomes a liberal cosmopolitan subject of globalization, a mobile world citizen at home at sea. Yet his race is the remainder of the colonial slavery that was not dissolved by legal emancipation, constituting the limit and critique of national enfranchisement; and unlike a MacQueen, in the midst of a storm threatening life and death, Equiano recognizes race, as a historical residue of colonial labor, in his expressed solidarity with the Black and creole workers and slaves onboard.

In a second scene, the manumitted Equiano bids farewell to his former master Robert King. King tells him that in a short time he will "have land and slaves of [your] own" (123) and pronounces the model of imperial subjectivity into which the former master instructs Equiano to aspire. In this sense, his education in arithmetic, navigation, accounting, and trading are critical parts of an imperial formation whose ultimate resolution is property ownership, and the imperial surveillance and management of others. The former slave is continuously interpellated by this imperial formation throughout the autobiography—from the initial chapter in which Equiano provides a protoethnographic description of African village life, to an account of Equiano's encounter with Indians on the Mosquito coast—yet inasmuch as he is hailed to assume an imperial subjectivity, the narrative simultaneously discloses its impossibility.

The episode that portrays Equiano's efforts to Christianize the Mosquito Indian prince provides a vivid illustration of the contradictions of the liberal autobiography. It first expresses that Equiano's accession to "freedom" is signified by his imitation of the white colonial posture toward the native peoples, and it demonstrates the obstacles that render impossible Equiano's realization of this position. Furthermore, the episode demonstrates that the liberal narrative of freedom overcoming enslavement both builds upon and continues to erase the ongoing settler seizure of lands, Christianization, and subordination of indigenous Americans. The Mosquito Indians were described by cartographers and buccaneers as an indigenous people in Central America, living along the coast that extends from Honduras to Nicaragua.[48] Equiano writes of his missionary zeal to convert "heathen" Indians to Christianity. When Equiano describes the Mosquito Indians as becoming "unruly" at a feast, he not only endorses corporal punishments for the native people, but Equiano identifies explicitly with the imperial explorer "Columbus": "I was so enraged with [the eighteen-year-old son of the Mosquito king], that I could have wished to have seen him tied fast to a tree and flogged for his behavior. . . . Recollecting a passage I had read in the life of Columbus, when he was amongst the Indians in Mexico or Peru, where, on some occasion, he frightened them by telling them of certain events in the heavens, I had recourse to the same expedient" (157). The narrative portrays Equiano emulating the stance of the European explorer when he points to the heavens, and threatens the native Mosquito people that he will menacingly "*tell* God to make them dead." Yet this conditional performance of identification is brief, for quite soon after, the autobiography recounts that Equiano was recaptured by British merchants; and taken prisoner, he was subsequently abused terribly by them. When he is once again free, and is kindly received by Indians, he comments: "They acted towards me more like Christians than those whites I was amongst the last night, though they had been baptized" (162). This episode in which Equiano attempts to perform his "freedom" by occupying the Englishman's position with respect to the Mosquito suggests that the liberal promise of freedom overcoming slavery reproduced a settler colonial relationship to native peoples. It emphasizes that although the history of African slaves and Mosquito peoples is entwined—Mosquitos were occasionally captured along with African slaves and sold in Jamaica, while they too often raided and traded African slaves—the history of indigenous Central Americans is far from identical to the history of transatlantic African slavery. Equiano's fleeting adoption of an imperial position with respect to the native Indian people, however contradicted by his vulnerability to capture and return to slavery, is an allegory of the degree to which liberal abolition reiterates settler colonialism, erasing indigenous difference.[49]

Finally, the contradiction between individual liberty and the persistence of collective slavery is most evident in the last episode of the autobiography, in which Equiano briefly recounts his participation in one of the first voyages to Sierra Leone, on behalf of the Committee for the Relief of the Black Poor to Resettle Poor Blacks and East Indians Living in England to Africa. Biographer Vincent Carretta suggests that the historical man named Equiano may have been the only person of African descent officially involved in the organization and administration of this actual historical project.[50] His stated wish to participate in this effort as a missionary who would convert Africans to Christianity would seem to conform to the colonial efforts to "bring civilization" to Africa, yet the narrator also reports feeling some reluctance and skepticism about the philanthropic nature of the project. Furthermore, his accusation of John Irwin, the agent in charge, of financial mismanagement and withholding provisions from the poor black settlers results in Equiano's immediate dismissal from his post and his return to England. He describes his journey to Sierra Leone as "an expedition, however unfortunate in the event . . . humane and politic in its design," but ultimately a "failure" (173). The "failure" of the Sierra Leone project is often conflated with the career of the individual man, and interpreted in terms of its confirmation of the persistence of racial barriers to Equiano's achievement of liberty; for example, Christine Levecq observes that the rhetoric used by the white philanthropists who dismissed Equiano tended to racialize Equiano's difference and to vilify his dissent as inciting black rebellion, and Ronald Paul concludes that the episode exposed the "racist nature of the British state and the precarious situation in which Equiano remained as a Black man."[51] Vincent Carretta mutes this "failure" by suggesting there is "little evidence supporting the contention that Equiano's dismissal was racially motivated" and gives his opinion that "Equiano and Irwin were both at fault," in that "Equiano did not go quietly."[52] Carretta emphasizes Equiano's "vindication" when *The Interesting Narrative* is published in 1789, and employed in the abolitionist campaign that later "successfully" brought a formal end to the slave trade in 1807.

Yet I propose that if we shift the emphasis of the analysis away from terms that the liberal narrative autobiography would seem to dictate—

that is, the success or failure of the individual subject Equiano—we can read the final "failure" as a quite necessary disclosure of the history of colonial slavery and empire. The declaration of "failure" marks a defining moment when historical contradictions break through the liberal genre of the individual's journey from slavery to freedom whose resolution would enact the suppression of ongoing colonial slavery. The "failure" is the very important sign that the genre of autobiography cannot resolve and contain the contradictions of slavery.

The Sierra Leone Resettlement of 1787–91, as envisioned by the abolitionist Granville Sharp, was a utopian experiment to bring "a community of free African settlers" to an outpost named the "Province of Freedom," in which they could be self-governing. Abolitionist Sharp had been known for having led the campaign that obtained the 1772 Mansfield ruling in the Somersett case, which established that former slave James Somersett, who had fled from America to Britain, was a free man, and could not be recaptured. The Somersett judgment, even if limited to prohibiting the forcible removal of slaves from England, established a precedent and was widely interpreted as outlawing slavery in England.[53] The Sierra Leone project expressed the abolitionists' desire to emancipate Blacks by means of resettling them in an African homeland. The plan's approval by Parliament may have also expressed a means to resettle the Blacks who had fought on the British side during the American Revolution as well as permitting slavery supporters to remove Blacks from Britain to an African colony secured in the British empire. Sharp declared in his *Short Sketch of Temporary Regulations for Sierra Leone*, "As soon as a slave shall set his foot within the bounds of the new settlement, he shall be deemed a *free man*."[54] Yet not only was the Province of Freedom short-lived—it lasted only four years from 1787 to 1791, but it "failed" in the larger sense that the vision of a state for emancipated Blacks in "free English territory in Africa" was far from fulfilled. In 1787, the time of the first expedition, reports disclosed insurmountable difficulties in the settlement— mortality, desertion, conflict—which continued once it came under the rule of the Sierra Leone Company from 1791 to 1807.[55] Sharp, Wilberforce, and Clarkson were the directors of the Sierra Leone Company, which governed and developed the colony populated by Blacks from Nova Scotia, the United States, and Jamaica, and Africans from the region; the first Reports of the Company Court of Directors detail disease, bad crops, great expenses, a war with France, and two insurrections by Nova Scotian Black settlers unhappy with the distribution of land. While participation in the slave trade was expressly forbidden by the Sierra Leone Company, not only did company employees engage in the slave trade, but many left company employment in order to become more engaged in the lucrative trade along the West African coast. Once the 1807 Slave Act abolished the trade throughout the empire, Sierra Leone became a Crown colony with a new critical role in the trade.[56]

The Slave Act had enormous consequences for Sierra Leone. While making the trade illegal, the act provided that British naval vessels could capture slave ships and provided for the trials of owners and crews before a British court. Paradoxically, laws that abolished the trade gave rise to a proliferation of new means and practices for transporting and trading slaves. For expediency, there were British courts set up on the West African coast, rather than in England, and Sierra Leone became one site for these trials. Some rationalized the British takeover of Sierra Leone, making it a Crown colony in 1808, in relation to the need for these courts and the necessity of trying those involved in the "illegal Traffick in Slaves"; possessing a harbor along the western coast of Africa, it was also a prime location for a British naval base as merchants sought to expand legitimate trades in ivory, palm oil, and cotton cloth. The British Navy policed the waters for illegal ships, and Vice Admiralty Courts were set up in Freetown, in Sierra Leone, to try offenders. The British Commissioners Gregory and Fitzgerald wrote to Foreign Secretary Canning in 1822 of the ongoing slave trade and reported "the range of Coast Southward from Sierra Leone to Cape Coast, the roads of *Gallinas* continue most prominently distinguished for constant and active Slave-trade . . . the total yearly export of about 3,000 slaves from *Gallinas*."[57] They detailed the cases adjudicated at Sierra Leone, the ships condemned, and slaves captured. The Gallinas country had been an important slave-trading center during the eighteenth century, reaching its peak in the second half. The abolition of the slave trade actually boosted the Gallinas trade, when the establishment of the Vice Admiralty Court made Freetown the center of the British Navy's suppression activities, and rendered Gallinas an attractive outpost.[58] The trade described by the British Commissioners might well have alluded to Pedro Blanco, a notorious Spanish slave trader based in Gallinas who began trading in African slaves in 1822, and who by 1839 controlled a network that imported slaves to work on Cuban plantations.[59] Blanco set up a *lomboko*, or a slave factory, a fortress stockade that consisted of several large holding depots or barracoons for slaves brought from the interior at the mouth of the Gallinas River, controlled by Spanish merchants within the then British colony; three thousand slaves a year were coming out of Gallinas River, with British observation and oversight, despite the fact that the trade was ostensibly illegal.

In their correspondence, the British Commissioners at Sierra Leone continually condemned the evils and treachery of the slave trade, but I read this correspondence *not* as evidence that the British legislation prohibiting the illegal trade actually stopped it, but to the contrary, that these documents and records about the prosecutions actually constitute evidence of the robust persistence and proliferation of the slave trade *after* 1807. That is, the 1807 Slave Act abolishing and prohibiting the trade did not bring the slave trade to an end, but rather its "illegality" actually elaborated the British forms of organization for regulating, documenting, and engaging with the trade. Moreover, it provided the conditions for the British to populate the Sierra Leone colony with "recaptives," the Africans "rescued" and "liberated" from illegal slave traders by the British.[60] Of the more than 100,000 African recaptives of diverse ethnic backgrounds "rescued" by the British Navy, over half were brought to Sierra Leone, baptized, and given Christian first and last names.[61] The British colony of Sierra Leone, which included captured slaves of diverse ethnic groups, Nova Scotian and American Blacks, Nigerians, other Africans, and migrants from Trinidad, Jamaica, and other West Indian islands, was not an experiment in freedom, but an exercise in social engineering, where the British sought to "civilize" Blacks through the establishment of schools, Christian religion, and inculcating an ethic of rewards and penalties—far from the initial vision of a state of free Black self-government. In addition, the British project of sending Blacks in England to Africa, many of whom had never before lived there, should be seen in context of expatriation projects as "final solutions" for maintaining white "racial purity" by deporting Blacks "back" to Africa in lieu of granting equality with whites. Many abolitionists in the United States at this time could understand Black emancipation only as a prelude to exile from American society. Thomas Jefferson, for example, in his 1787 *Notes on the State of Virginia*, famously made the removal of Blacks from the United States an integral part of a gradual emancipation scheme of education, emancipation (after the age of forty-five, to repay the slaveholder's investment), and expatriation to locations in Africa.[62]

Ultimately, Equiano's "failure" and his involvement with Sierra Leone's history expressed the larger contradictions of the eighteenth- and early nineteenth-century Atlantic world. The resettlement project promised to Black diaspora subjects the "return" to an Africa they had never known in order to secure some version of "freedom," yet to do so meant becoming a subject or object of Western colonial conquest of the region. The slave trade died a very slow death over the course of the nineteenth century, and the numbers of slave exports remained high. The British Anti-Slave Trade Squadron and Vice Admiralty Court in Sierra Leone seized and prosecuted ships belonging not only to British and U.S. traders, but more frequently to French, Portuguese, Spanish, and Dutch. Yet the anti–slave trade and antislavery agenda became a powerful pretext for the expansion of Britain's colonial interventions in Africa, accompanied by the shift to "legitimate" trades with African merchants. Ironically, Equiano became a most eloquent promoter of this economic thinking that advocated for trade with Africa, and indeed, *The Interesting Narrative* ends with Equiano's recommendation that the best solution to the abolition of slavery is the expansion of trade between Britain and Africa:

> A commercial intercourse with Africa opens an inexhaustible source of wealth to the manufacturing interests of Great Britain, and to all which the slave trade is an objection....

> I hope the slave trade will be abolished. I pray it may be an event at hand. The great body of manufacturers, uniting in the cause, will considerably facilitate and expedite it....If the blacks were permitted to remain in their own country, they would double themselves every fifteen years. In proportion to such increase will be the demand for manufactures. Cotton and indigo grow spontaneously in most parts of Africa; a consideration this of no small consequence to the manufacturing towns of Great Britain. It opens a most immense, glorious, and happy prospect—the clothing, &c. of a continent ten thousand miles in circumference, and immensely rich in the production of every denomination in return for manufactures. (177–78)

The final words of the autobiography thus voice the convergence of abolition with new circuits of trade and express the imbrication of the desire for freedom with expanded commerce. Equiano's "solution" to the struggle against the iniquities of slavery not only reiterates an understanding of Black emancipation as Black removal to Africa, but it anticipates precisely the British shift from eighteenth-century mercantilism and colonial slavery toward the new forms of empire that enabled the global expansion of trade in manufactured goods in the nineteenth century. Equiano names the conjunction of the abolition of slavery with the expansion of the British empire, and recommends that controlling circuits of worldwide commerce could be a more effective and profitable mode than the restricted gains of direct territorial conquest and colonial slavery. By connecting abolition with international "free trade," Equiano outlined the design for a new era of capitalist empire that was perfectly commensurate with the vision of administrators in the British Colonial and Foreign Offices who commissioned Kenneth MacQueen's 1807 voyage to China. In this sense, *The Interesting Narrative* mediated precisely the convergence of liberal abolition with imperial expansion into Asia and Africa, linking older geographies of conquest with new forms of sovereignty elaborated through commerce, trade, and movement across the seas. In the next chapters, I discuss the stakes of the early nineteenth-century debate about "free trade" in relation to the British East India Company monopoly and argue that the "opening" of the trades in India and China provided the conditions for the innovation of new forms of liberal governance and imperial security. The opening of free trade inaugurated the vast expansion that founded the British empire and endured until the end of the century.

Equiano's *Interesting Narrative* was a transatlantic life "translated" through the languages and institutions of liberal freedom; his "model migration" from Africa to the Americas and exemplary assimilation into modern literature, politics, and economy affirmed liberal promises of freedom; such promises subsumed the transatlantic world whose peoples, lands, and labor were the conditions of possibility for that freedom.

In effect, liberal genres, like the autobiography, reiterate a colonial division of humanity through this formalism of affirmation and forgetting, however much race is the remainder that continues to mark the limits to freedom for the subject of colonial slavery. In *The Interesting Narrative*, Equiano's relationship to freedom is forever haunted by his former status as property within transatlantic social relations. His affirmation of the desire for political economic right exists simultaneously with the forgetting of the ongoing condition of collective enslavement. Yet even as the autobiographical genre develops the self-authoring individual out of the transatlantic conditions, the text's digressions, heterogeneity, and contradictions permit us to read "against the grain" of this development.

I began the discussion of Equiano's autobiography with Britain's introduction of Chinese contract laborers to the West Indies in order to situate the introduction of Asian labor and the East Indies trades as crucial elements in the history of abolition of the slave trade, Black emancipation, and colonialism in Africa. While some might consider Colonial Office documents on Chinese labor in the Americas an unlikely archive to read alongside Equiano's autobiography, the papers offer a unique window onto colonial administrators' developing ideas about the abolition of African slavery within the limitations of mercantilism, and the expansion of free trade with markets beyond the West Indies that led to the extension of British colonialism in Africa. Likewise, the colonial papers on Sierra Leone might seem a distant, contiguous archive with little relevance to the East India Company trade with China and the opening of the "coolie" trade. Yet one can observe a relationship between the choice of Sierra Leone for a Crown colony in 1808, to and from whose port "recaptive" slaves were conveyed, and the considerations that led to the establishment of a Crown colony in Hong Kong in 1842 as a major point of arrival and departure for ships carrying Chinese workers around the world; the early command of trade through governing the port at Sierra Leone was a strategy greatly elaborated in the middle and latter parts of the nineteenth century in Hong Kong and coastal China. In other words, to interpret Equiano's autobiography as a seamless narrative of slavery to freedom within the historical context of the British abolition of the slave trade is to radically restrict its scope and meaning, and to discipline it in terms of narrowly construed imperatives of the genre. It is to fix and bind the narrative in time and place, in the same manner that the imperial drive of the colonial archive would appear to regulate the meanings of the documents it contains. We might instead take generous "detours around proper knowledge" into the "territories of failure," by combining unlikely archives, reading Equiano in relation to the 1803 "Secret Memorandum," and by considering the Sierra Leone court prosecutions of illegal traffickers in relation to the Second Governor of Hong Kong's criminal laws against unregistered vagrants.[63] We might connect *The Interesting Narrative* not only to the seventeenth-century transatlantic African slave trade and the European colonial development of plantation production in the Americas, but also to the settlers' conquests of lands and wars with native peoples, and to the nineteenth-century "transition from slavery to free labor" in which Chinese and Indians were recruited to British, French, and Spanish colonies throughout the Caribbean and Latin America. The longevity of Equiano's autobiography is evidence of the resilience of desire for the representative individual story of the achievement of freedom, but let us dedicate our reading practices to connecting that individual story to the more extensive intimacies of four continents that gave rise to the modern narrative of the singular life.

1 See Kenneth R. Andrews, *Trade, Plunder, and Settlement: Maritime Enterprise and the Genesis of the British Empire, 1480–1630* (Cambridge: Cambridge University Press, 1985); Peter Linebaugh and Marcus Rediker, *The Many-Headed Hydra: Sailors, Slaves, Commoners, and the Hidden History of the Revolutionary Atlantic* (Boston: Beacon, 2000); David Kazanjian, *The Colonizing Trick: National Culture and Imperial Citizenship in Early America* (Minneapolis: University of Minnesota Press, 2003); Lauren Benton, A *Search for Sovereignty: Law and Geography in European Empires, 1400–1900* (Cambridge: Cambridge University Press, 2009).

2 Felicity A. Nussbaum, ed., *The Global Eighteenth Century* (Baltimore: Johns Hopkins University Press, 2003); Carl Schmitt, *The Nomos of the Earth in the International Law of the Jus Publicum Europaeum*, trans. G. L. Ulmen [1950] (New York: Telos, 2006). Schmitt discussed the "*nomos* of the earth" as the shifting international order within which the nation-state emerged, expressing the liberal desire for unfettered expansion founded on the imagination of the "New World" as an open horizon, at once excluded from and constitutive of the order of international law.

3 Great Britain Colonial Office Correspondence, co 295, vol. 17.

4 David Eltis, *Economic Growth and the End of the Transatlantic Slave Trade* (New York: Oxford University Press, 1987).

5 In "A Brief View of the Nature and Effects of Negro Slavery, as it exists in the Colonies of Great Britain," *Westminster Review* (1830) editors endorse the Statement by the Committee of the Society for the Abolition of Slavery throughout the British Dominions.

6 For example, Seymour Drescher, *From Slavery to Freedom: Comparative Studies in the Rise and Fall of Atlantic Slavery* (Basingstoke, UK: Macmillan, 1999); David Eltis, Frank D. Lewis, Kenneth L. Sokoloff, eds., *Slavery in the Development of the Americas* (Cambridge: Cambridge University Press, 2004). Much work complicates the assumption of transition: see, for example, Frederick Cooper, Thomas C. Holt, Rebecca J. Scott, eds., *Beyond Slavery: Explorations of Race, Labor, and Citizenship in Postemancipation Societies* (Chapel Hill: University of North Carolina Press, 2000); Thomas Holt, *The Problem of Freedom: Race, Labor and Politics in Jamaica and Britain, 1832–1938* (Baltimore: Johns Hopkins University Press, 1992); Demetrius Eudell, *The Political Language of Emancipation in the British Caribbean and the U.S. South* (Chapel Hill: University North Carolina Press, 2002).

7 On the transatlantic slave trade and slavery system, see Orlando Patterson, *The Sociology of Slavery: An Analysis of the Origins, Development and Structure of Negro Slave Society in Jamaica* (Rutherford, NJ: Fairleigh Dickinson, 1975); Herbert Klein, *Slavery in the Americas* (Chicago: University of Chicago Press, 1967); Philip D. Curtin, *The Atlantic Slave Trade: A Census* (Madison: University of Wisconsin Press, 1969); David Brion Davis, *Slavery and Human Progress* (Oxford: Oxford University Press, 1984); David Eltis, *Economic Growth and the Ending of the Transatlantic Slave Trade* (Oxford: Oxford University Press, 1987); Walter Johnson, *Soul by Soul: Life Inside the Antebellum Slave Market* (Cambridge, MA: Harvard University Press, 1999); Saidiya Hartman, *Scenes of Subjection: Terror, Slavery, and Self-Making in the Nineteenth Century* (Oxford: Oxford University Press, 1997); Stephanie Smallwood, *Saltwater Slavery: A Middle Passage from Africa to American Diaspora* (Cambridge, MA: Harvard University Press, 2007).

8 Houston A. Baker Jr., *Blues, Ideology, and Afro-American Literature: A Vernacular Theory* (Chicago: University of Chicago Press, 1984), 33.

9 See Paul Gilroy, *The Black Atlantic: Modernity and Double Consciousness* (Cambridge, MA: Harvard University Press,

1993); Joseph Roach, *Cities of the Dead: Circum-Atlantic Performance* (New York: Columbia University Press, 1996); Peter Linebaugh and Marcus Rediker, *The Many-Headed Hydra: Sailors, Slaves, Commoners, and the Hidden History of the Revolutionary Atlantic* (Boston: Beacon, 2000); Ian Baucom, ed., "*Atlantic Genealogies*," special double issue of *South Atlantic Quarterly* (spring/summer 2001); Alan Rice, *Radical Narratives of the Black Atlantic* (London: Continuum, 2003); Felicity Nussbaum, ed., *The Global Eighteenth Century* (Baltimore: Johns Hopkins University Press, 2003); Pamela Scully and Diane Paton, eds., *Gender and Slave Emancipation in the Atlantic World* (Durham, NC: Duke University Press, 2005); Ian Baucom, *Specters of the Atlantic: Finance Capital, Slavery, and the Philosophy of History* (Durham, NC: Duke University Press, 2005). Laura Doyle, *Freedom's Empire: Race and the Rise of the Novel in Atlantic Modernity, 1640–1940* (Durham, NC: Duke University Press, 2008).

10 Cathy N. Davidson, "Olaudah Equiano, Written by Himself," *Novel* 40, no. 1/2 (fall 2006): 18–51, 19.

11 *The Speech of William Wilberforce*, Esq., *Representative of York, on Wednesday the 13th of May, 1789, on the Question of the Abolition of the Slave Trade* (London: Logographic Press, 1789), 12–13. For other key voices in the British abolition debate, see Peter J. Kitson, ed. *Slavery, Abolition, and Emancipation: The Abolition Debate* (London: Pickering and Chatto, 1999).

12 Biographer Vincent Carretta unearthed documents that suggest that a"Gustavus Vassa" may have been born in Carolina rather than Africa, inaugurating a discussion of the possibility that Equiano may have invented his Igbo origins as fiction rather than reclaimed the accounts of Africa and the Middle Passage. See Vincent Carretta, "Olaudah Equiano or Gustavus Vassa? New Light on an Eighteenth-Century Question of Identity," *Slavery and Abolition* 20, no. 3 (December 1999): 96–105. My discussion addresses the cultural and social force of Equiano's *Interesting Narrative* as a canonical work that has been taken to describe African origins, the Middle Passage, and slavery in the Americas, through which ongoing interests in colonial slavery and abolition were mediated, in the time of its publication and in subsequent receptions; in this sense, the ambiguity of birth is of less significance than the meaning of the autobiography. Indeed, Carretta described Equiano as "the first successful professional writer of African descent in the English-speaking world." Vincent Carretta, *Equiano, The African: Biography of a Self-Made Man* (Athens: University of Georgia Press, 2005), 366.

Carretta's discovery has given rise to numerous rejoinders from historians. For example, Andrew Byrd asserts that the autobiography's expression of Igbo culture "actually suggests someone deeply familiar with and in some way affected by the social and political geography of the Biafran interior," and "whatever Vassa's origins, the ethnographic language of his memoir supplies good internal evidence that the origins of *The Interesting Narrative* lie decidedly in the Biafran interior and were profoundly African" (125). Andrew X. Byrd, "Eboe, Country, Nation, and Gustavus Vassa's 'Interesting Narrative,'" *William and Mary Quarterly*, 3rd ser., 63, no. 1 (January 2006): 123–48.

13 See Benjamin Franklin, *Autobiography: An Authoritative Text, Background, Criticisms* [1793], ed. J. A. Leo Lemay and P. M. Zall (New York: W. W. Norton, 1986); Mitchell Breitwieser, *Cotton Mather and Benjamin Franklin: The Price of Representative Personality* (Cambridge: Cambridge University Press, 1984); Michael Warner, *The Letters of the Republic: Publication and the Public Sphere in Eighteenth-Century America* (Cambridge, MA: Harvard University Press, 1990); Nancy Armstrong and Leonard Tennenhouse, *The Imaginary Puritan: Literature, Intellectual Labor, and the Origins of Personal Life* (Berkeley: University of California Press, 1994); Trish Loughron, *The Republic in Print: Print Culture in the Age of U.S. Nation Building, 1770–1870* (New York: Columbia University Press, 2007).

14 Aphra Behn, *Oroonoko*, ed. Joanna Lipking (New York: W. W. Norton, 1977), 13.

15 Chi-ming Yang, "Asia Out of Place," *Eighteenth-Century Studies* 42, no. 1 (2008): 235–53.

16 Srinivas Aravamudan, *Tropicopolitans: Colonialism and Agency, 1688–1804* (Durham, NC: Duke University Press, 1999).

17 Adam Smith, *Theory of Moral Sentiments* [1759] (Oxford University Press, 1996), 9.

18 On sentimentalism and antislavery discourse, see Christine Levecq, *Slavery and Sentiment: The Politics of Feeling in Black Atlantic Slavery Writing, 1770–1850* (Durham: University of New Hampshire Press, 2008).

19 See Lynn Festa, *Sentimental Figures of Empire in Eighteenth-Century Britain and France* (Baltimore: Johns Hopkins University Press, 2006); Shirley Samuels, ed., *The Culture of Sentiment: Race, Gender, and Sentimentality* (Oxford: Oxford University Press, 1992); Shelley Streeby, *American Sensations: Class, Empire, and the Production of Popular Culture* (Berkeley: University of California Press, 2002); Elizabeth Dillon, *The Gender of Freedom: Fictions of Liberalism and the Literary Public Sphere* (Stanford, CA: Stanford University Press, 2004).

20 Thomas Bicknell and John Day, *The Dying Negro* (London: W. Flexney, 1775).

21 Festa, *Sentimental*, 2.

22 The original two volumes of *The Interesting Narrative of the Life of Olaudah Equiano, or Gustavus Vassa, the African, Written by Himself*, printed and sold for the author by T. Elkins, London, in 1789, included an engraved portrait of Equiano, wearing a formal dress coat, holding in his right hand a Bible. Across from the title page, it begins with a letter addressed to "The Lords Spiritual and Temporal, and the Commons of the Parliament of Great Britain," and is prefaced with the list of subscribers, endorsing the autobiography.

All page citations from Werner Sollers, ed., *The Interesting Narrative of the Life of Olaudah Equiano, or Gustavus Vassa, the African, Written by Himself* [1789] (New York: W. W. Norton, 2001), 39.

23 Gerard Genette, *Narrative Discourse: An Essay in Method*, trans. Jane E. Lewin (Ithaca, NY: Cornell University Press, 1980).

24 Henry Louis Gates Jr. and William L. Andrews, eds. *Pioneers of the Black Atlantic: Five Slave Narratives from the Enlightenment*, 1772–1815 (Washington, DC: Civitas, 1998).

25 William Louis Stern, "The Uses of Botany, with Special Reference to the 18th Century," *Taxon* 42, no. 4 (November 1993): 773–79.

26 Cugoano was captured in his native Ghana, sold into slavery, and taken to Grenada, then purchased by an Englishman for whom he became a servant; in England he became a freedman, and by 1786 emerged as a leader of the black poor in London. Ottobah Cugoano, *Thoughts and sentiments on the evil and wicked traffic of the slavery and commerce of the human species: humbly submitted to the inhabitants of Great-Britain* [1787], in Henry Louis Gates Jr. and William L. Andrews, eds. *Pioneers of the Black Atlantic*, 83–183. On Cugoano, see Saidiya V. Hartman, *Lose Your Mother: A Journey along the Atlantic Slave Route* (New York: Farrar, 2008), 121–22; Roxane Wheeler, " 'Betrayed by Some of My Own Complexion': Cugoano, Abolition, and the Contemporary Language of Racialism," in *Genius in Bondage*, ed. V. Carretta and P. Gould (Lexington: University Press of Kentucky, 2001), 17–38.

27 William Andrews, *To Tell a Free Story: First Century of Afro-American Autobiography, 1760–1865* (Urbana: University of Illinois Press, 1986).

28 Fred Moten, *In the Break: The Aesthetics of the Black Radical Tradition* (Minneapolis: University of Minnesota Press, 2003).

29 Henry Louis Gates Jr. and William L. Andrews, eds., *Pioneers of the Black Atlantic*.

30 Frances Smith Foster, *Witnessing Slavery: The Development of the Ante-bellum Slave Narrative*, 2nd ed. (University of Wisconsin Press, 1994).

31 Henry Louis Gates Jr., *The Signifying Monkey: A Theory of African American Literary Criticism* (New York: Oxford University Press, 1988).

32 Andrews, *To Tell a Free Story*, 32–33.

33 See Robert Stepto, *From behind the Veil: A Study of Afro-American Narrative* (Urbana: University of Illinois Press, 1979); John Sekora, "Black Message/ White Envelope: *Genre, Authenticity, and Authority in the Antebellum Slave Narrative*," *Callaloo* 32 (summer 1987): 482–515.

34 As in Fredrick Douglass's famous *chiasmus*: "You have seen how a man was made a slave; you shall see how a slave was made a man." Frederick Douglass, *Narrative of the Life of Frederick Douglass, An American Slave*, introduction by Kwame Anthony Appiah (New York: Random House, 2000). See also Deborah McDowell's "In the First Place: Making Frederick Douglass and the Afro-American Narrative Tradition," in William Andrews, ed. *Critical Essays on Frederick Douglass* (Boston: G. K. Hall, 1991), 192–214.

35 Fred Moten, *In the Break*.

36 Hazel Carby, "Becoming Modern Racialized Subjects: Detours through Our Pasts to Produce Ourselves Anew," *Cultural Studies* 23, no. 4 (2009): 634.

37 Aravamudan, *Tropicolitans*; see also Srinivas Aravamudan, "Equiano Lite," *Eighteenth-Century Studies 34*, no. 4 (2001): 615–19; Christine Leveqc, "Sentiment and Cosmopolitanism in Olaudah Equiano's Narrative," *African and Black Diaspora: An International Journal* 1, no. 1 (2008): 13–30.

38 Cathy Davidson discusses the "hybrid form" of Equiano's *Interesting Narrative* as resembling many eighteenth-century novels (both American and European), "a conscious shaping of myriad life-events into recognizable plot patterns." Davidson, "Olaudah Equiano," 19.

39 See Ronald Paul, " 'I Whitened My Face That They Might Not Know Me': Race and Identity in Olaudah Equiano's Slave Narrative." *Journal of Black Studies* 39, no. 6 (2009): 848–64.

40 Carby, "Becoming Modern Racialized Subjects," 634.

41 Aravamudan, *Tropicolitans*, 253.

42 Walter Johnson, "Time and Revolution in African America," in *Rethinking American History in a Global Age*, ed. Thomas Bender (Berkeley: University of California Press, 2002), 152.

43 Stephanie Smallwood, *Saltwater Slavery*, 122.

44 Saidiya Hartman, "The Time of Slavery," *South Atlantic Quarterly* 100, no. 4 (fall 2002): 757–77; and Saidiya V. Hartman, *Lose Your Mother*.

45 See also Saidiya V. Hartman, *Scenes of Subjection*.

46 Vincent Carretta, *Equiano*.

47 David Kazanjian, "Race, Nation, and Equality: Olauhah Equiano's *Interesting Narrative* and a Genealogy of U.S. Mercantilism," in *Post-nationalist American Studies*, ed. John Carlos Rowe et al. (Berkeley: University of California Press, 2000), 131; also Kazanjian, *The Colonizing Trick*.

48 The Mosquito coast extended about five hundred

miles along the Caribbean Sea east along the coast of modern Honduras to the northeastern tip of present-day Nicaragua, and south to what is now Costa Rica; in the eighteenth century, control was disputed between the British and Spanish. See John Baily, *Central America; Describing Each of the States of Guatemala, Honduras, Salvador, Nicaragua, and Costa Rica* (London: Trelawney Saunders, 1850). There is a long history of frequent contacts of Mosquito Indians with British colonists in Jamaica, which included social and cultural mixing with settlers and slaves, some Mosquito enslavement as well as some Mosquito adoption of European practices of capturing Black slaves to be kept or sold; in 1728, the buccaneer and author M.W. described the Mosquito as mixed or "Zambo," and presentday Mosquito people are classified as of African-Native descent. See Mary W. Helms, "Miskito Slaving and Culture Contact: Ethnicity and Opportunity in an Expanding Population," *Journal of Anthropological Research* 39, no. 2 (summer 1983): 179–97.

49 Specifying the history of settler appropriation of indigenous lands, knowledges, and histories, indigenous studies scholars urge an analysis of colonial capitalism that nuances settler colonial seizure, appropriation, and removal as different from paradigms that center racial slavery or racialized labor, cautioning that adoption of liberal ideas of rights and sovereignty often reiterates this settler violence. See Jodi A. Byrd, *The Transit of Empire: Indigenous Critiques of Colonialism* (Minneapolis: University of Minnesota Press, 2011); Shona N. Jackson, *Creole Indigeneity: Between Myth and the Nation in the Caribbean* (Minneapolis: University of Minnesota Press, 2012); Glen Coulthard, "From Wards of the State to Subjects of Recognition? Marx, Indigenous Peoples, and the Politics of Dispossession in Denedeh," in Audra Simpson and Andrea Smith, eds., *Theorizing Native Studies* (Durham, NC: Duke University Press, 2014), 56–98; Manu Vimalassery, "The Prose of Counter-Sovereignty," in Alyosha Goldstein, ed. *Formations of United States Colonialism* (Durham, NC: Duke University Press, 2014).

50 Carretta, *Equiano*, 225.

51 Levecq, "Sentiment," 26; Paul, " 'I Whitened,' " 861.

52 Carretta, *Equiano*, 229.

53 On the Somerset case, see *English Historical Documents*, vol. 10, ed. D. C. Douglas, D. B. Horn, and M. Ransome (London: Eyre and Spottiswoode, 1953); Stephen Usherwood, "The Black Must Be Discharged: The Abolitionists' Debt to Lord Mansfield," *History Today* 31, no. 3 (March 1981): 40–45.

Later in 1783, the historical Equiano had told Granville Sharp of the events aboard the *Zong*, when 133 slaves were killed en masse so that the ship owners could seek insurance compensation for their "lost cargo," which prompted Sharp to become involved. On this notorious event, see James Walvin, *The Zong: A Massacre, the Law and the End of Slavery* (New Haven, CT: Yale University Press, 2011); Baucom, Specters of the Atlantic; and the poetic rendering, M. NourbeSe Phillip, *Zong!* (Middletown, CT: Wesleyan University Press, 2011).

54 Granville Sharp, *Short Sketch of Temporary Regulations (until Better Shall Be Proposed) for the Intended Settlement on the Grain Coast of Africa, near Sierra Leona* (London: H. Baldwin, Fleet-Street, 1786), 22.

Historians point out that the "black" settlers in Sierra Leone were actually a heterogeneous group of Africans, East Indians, Afro-Americans, and white Britons; the initial settlement would include former Virginians, Carolinians, other refugees of the American war from Nova Scotia, and later "recaptives," or slaves captured from illegal slave ships after 1807.

55 HCPP *Report from the Committee on Petition of the Court of Directors of the Sierra Leone Company* (May 1802).

56 For a comprehensive history of nineteenth-century Sierra Leone, see Christopher Fyfe, *A History of Sierra Leone* (Oxford: Oxford University Press, 1962); on the history of the Sierra Leone Resettlement project, see Alexander X. Byrd, *Captives and Voyagers: Black Migrants across the Eighteenth-Century British Atlantic World* (Baton Rouge: Louisiana State University Press, 2008).

57 HCPP ,"Correspondence with the British commissioners, at Sierra Leone, the Havannah, Rio de Janeiro, and Surinam, relating to the slave trade," 6–7.

58 Adam Jones, *From Slaves to Palm Kernels: A History of the Galinhas Country (West Africa), 1730–1890* (Wiesbaden: Steiner, 1983).

59 Jones, *From Slaves*, 42–44, 50–51.

60 Parliamentary Papers collected accounts of all vessels seized, captured, or detained for illegal traffic in slaves, documents pertaining to their trials in the Commission Courts, and records of the numbers of slaves captured and "emancipated." See HCPP 1822, "Vessels captured, and Vessels Condemned"; HCPP 1823, "Correspondence with the British commissioners, at Sierra Leone, the Havannah, Rio de Janeiro, and Surinam, relating to the slave trade," for example, "List of Cases Adjudged in the Courts of Mixed Commission at Sierra Leone, between the 1st of January 1822 and the 1st of January 1823," 14.

61 Johnson Asiegbu, *Slavery and the Politics of Liberation 1787–1861: A Study of Liberated African Emigration and British Anti-slavery Policy* (New York: Africana Publishers, 1969); Rosanne Marion Adderley, *"New Negroes from Africa": Slave Trade Abolition and Free African Settlement* (Bloomington: Indiana University Press, 2006).

62 Thomas Jefferson, *Notes on the State of Virginia* [1787] (Baltimore: W. Pechin, 1800).

63 On "failure" as a critical project see Judith Halberstam, *The Queer Art of Failure* (Durham, NC: Duke University Press, 2011), 25.

Settler Entanglements from Citrus Production to Historical Memory

Muriam Haleh Davis

in *Middle East Report* 302, 51,
no. 1 (Spring 2022)

All architects of settler colonies have been obsessed with land: who occupies it, how it is cultivated and what forms of labor are required to make it productive. In the nineteenth century the issue of how to manage colonized lands led imperial powers to introduce various economic and legal structures and construct new racial hierarchies in response to the unique challenges of each territory. Colonists introduced (or transformed) conceptions of racial difference, contended with specific environmental obstacles borne of local ecologies and navigated competing metropolitan ideas about colonization. Sometimes, studying a single commodity such as citrus can shed light on how a common set of tropes and strategies structured these disparate approaches. By introducing new forms of agriculture, settlers often expressed a drive to remake the landscape and promised moral as well as economic advancement to the subjects they colonized—even though the possibility of physical or cultural elimination of Indigenous groups was an ever-present threat.

Individuals who participated in fashioning settler colonies, along with their metropolitan supporters, often lay claim to a form of exceptionalism. The United States couched its supposed uniqueness in terms of a city on a hill, the Zionist movement points to the status of Jews as a "chosen people" and France boasted the promises of the civilizing mission. Settler colonial regimes past and present have devised rhetorical strategies to distinguish their own system of rule from others, to disavow the structural violence of settlement that is common to them all and to obscure a set of broader relationships.

They are, however, not exceptional. Disparate settler colonial regimes are entangled with each other; they continue to be established and sustained by ideological, economic and political strategies that developed in a transnational framework. Ignoring these connections or examining settler-colonial regimes as discrete case studies has political consequences. This approach undermines the analysis of settler colonialism as a structure that was developed across national borders and allows contemporary debates to focus on settler colonialism as a discrete event, rather than historical structure. For historian Patrick Wolfe, settler colonialism is a structure, not an event, meaning that the project should be defined by long-term contests for land rather than the initial violence of conquest.[1] It is perhaps unsurprising, therefore, that communities fighting against settler colonialism often deliberately highlight the commonalities between regimes as a tool to build solidarity.

Shared Ideological Tropes

The settlers, politicians and planners who were invested in the project of colonization participated in a global discussion on race, land and political economy. They viewed their activities through a common set of ideological tropes, making sense of their policies in a comparative framework. For example, as French colonial planners and politicians debated various possibilities for what to do with the Algerians following the conquest in 1830—including extermination, resettlement and assimilation—they often referenced the United States. Eugène Bodichon, a progressive republican who wrote frequently on Algerian policy in the 1830s, believed that the Algerians would experience a fate similar to the "auto-genocide" of the American Indians. This theme was popularized in French literary narratives in the first half of the nineteenth century.[2] Similarly, early Zionists in Palestine saw manual labor and agriculture as having a redemptive value and modeled their settlements on France's colonization of Algeria.[3]

Different settler colonial projects drew upon similar concepts to sustain the myths of their own indigeneity and self-sufficiency. By the end of the nineteenth century, close to 700,000 Europeans lived in Algeria. These new arrivals not only took most of the fertile land for their own use, they also claimed the moniker of "Algerian" for themselves. (Actual Algerians were pejoratively referred to as "natives," Muslims or Jews.) European Algerians' self-ascribed identity as hardy pioneers bore similarities to identities common in the Yishuv, the Zionist movement's name for the Jewish settler community in Palestine before Israel's establishment in 1948. In the late nineteenth century, many Jews who settled in Ottoman Palestine after fleeing antisemitism in Eastern Europe were fascinated by the figure of the cowboy, that mythical figure who embodied the virtues of chivalry and generosity and bore traces of rebellion and rugged individualism. William Frederick Cody (known as Buffalo Bill) drew enormous crowds in Paris at the 1889 *Exposition Universelle* and inspired articles in Algerian newspapers. Theodor Herzl himself compared Jewish riders in Palestine to cowboys during an 1898 visit to the region.[4] This pioneer identity underpinned the fantasy of self-sufficiency held by the Europeans who settled in Algeria even as the colonial state provided the credit, land and infrastructure required for the large-scale industrialized agriculture they needed to prosper.

Citrus and Settlement

In the nineteenth century, citrus (in addition to wine) came to symbolize the landscapes of settler colonies. Large-scale citrus production in the United States, Palestine and Algeria informed settler identity, shaped discourses about the land and created connections between settler colonies established by different countries. The development of a citrus industry required extensive state investment in credit and the construction of dams. It also relied on a host of technologies that ensured the standardization, preservation and shipping of delicate fruit—processes that were made possible by global capitalist integration in the late nineteenth century.

Settlers in California, Algeria and Palestine intensified the cultivation of this typically Mediterranean commodity upon their arrival. In the 1830s, citrus farms occupied just 420 acres of the Algerian countryside. By the 1950s that figure had reached 61,750.[5] While Palestinian citriculture pre-dated the arrival of Jewish settlers, especially around Jaffa, the rapid development of dams and the expansion of European markets caused Jewish citrus production to increase exponentially under the British Mandate (1920–1948). Similarly, California experienced a "citrus rush" from 1890 to 1945 that generated more income than the better-known gold rush.

Colonial planners in all three territories drew connections between citriculture and what they called "Mediterranean civilization"—not only through physical transformation of the landscapes, but also by participating in creating the idea of a new Mediterranean race. In both Algeria and the Yishuv, intellectuals proclaimed a local vernacular of Mediterranean identity from the 1930s to the 1950s—such as Albert Camus' "Mediterranean humanism" or the notion of a "Mediterranean option" that was invoked by Israeli artists and writers to naturalize their presence on the land.[6] In the United States, it is still possible to read tourist guides in California boasting of how oranges "transformed the deserts of Southern California into a Mediterranean Oasis."[7]

Despite these ideological renderings, citrus production was less a sign of a new mode of (mythical) Mediterranean co-existence than the product of a racialized system of labor. In California, Chinese, Japanese and Indigenous men provided cheap labor from the mid-1890s through 1914, though they were replaced by Mexican laborers after World War I.[8] Jewish citrus farmers in Palestine continued to employ low-paid native Palestinian Arabs even after the birth of the Labor Zionist campaign to "conquer" Palestine's labor market for Jewish immigrants. This racial capitalist logic also underpinned citriculture in Algeria, where Muslim laborers carried out many of the manual tasks and helped keep costs down on French orchards.

Commonalities among labor practices, and the use of racial categories as an organizing principle for recruitment, are not the only ways in which citrus offers a window into how settler colonial regimes employed similar tactics. Discrepant settler colonial projects were also enmeshed through their citrus industries' promotion and circulation of scientific knowledge. Agronomists in the Yishuv and Algeria (as well as Morocco) studied California's experience with citrus from the interwar period through decolonization in the late 1950s. French and Zionist planners visited the Golden State, bringing back technical ideas and political optimism. As one French planner who traveled to the United States wrote in 1932, thanks to irrigation the government could hope for an "influx of French farmers, of workers, of small capitalists, [all] attracted by the new evolution of Algeria that will be populated by more French nationals and that will become a real extension of France."[9]

In the early years after the 1948 Nakba—the expulsion of Palestinians from their land and homes by Zionist forces—and the establishment of Israel, citrus became a venue for French cooperation with the nascent state. When the National School of Agriculture in Algiers sent students to Israel to study citrus farming in 1958, the official report noted that despite the country's "isolation in the midst of a hostile world that unites its forces [planning] for future attacks," Israel "knows what it wants and has faith in its future."[10] This description was clearly meant as a partial explanation of why Israel had been chosen as the site for this visit. The report also invoked Herzl and his belief that a "new race of Jews" would emerge from the soil.[11] These shared imaginaries continued during decolonization, as some French politicians in the 1950s viewed Israel as a model for partitioning Algerian territory into separate French and "Arab" states. Later in the decade, Israeli officials depicted Palestinian citizens who agitated against the state's restrictions on their movement, employment and political rights (and who analyzed these policies in a broader settler-colonial context) as would-be Algerian rebels.[12]

Settler Fantasies of Reconciliation

The large-scale production of citrus is just one example of the myriad links—both economic and ideological—that bound different settler-colonial projects. These ties were multiple; they included a common set of cultural imaginaries, economic practices and geographical commitments. Yet despite these similarities, some observers continue to depict their own national history of settler colonialism as singular. This focus on the exceptional nature of a particular settler colony serves to obscure the transcolonial reality of empire as it developed in the nineteenth and early twentieth centuries.

The question of whether settler colonies should be studied in isolation or across space and time is not an arcane matter of academic methodology. Contemporary commentators on colonial history (especially those with links to the state) are not merely demonstrating a lack of curiosity or historical myopia in insisting on a national frame. Instead, the assertion of exceptionality can be read as a particular kind of settler fantasy that promises an easier path to reconciliation.[13] Reconciliation can be defined as an attempt to make discrepant views of history compatible, therefore ending acrimonious debates surrounding historical memory. A second definition, of restoring amicable relations between colonial perpetrators and their victims, is also relevant. In both cases, settler-colonial states are keen to "move on" from debates on colonial crimes, seeking ways to avoid the messy work of introducing social justice in the wake of decolonization. By insisting that the history of France (or Israel or the United States) is entirely unique, analysts obscure the broader structural questions at the heart of settlement. Observers should understand contemporary analyses of settler colonialism that focus on the event (rather than structure) of decolonization in light of the fantasy that reconciliation is possible, or even desirable.

In recent years French President Emmanuel Macron has initiated an official policy that seeks a "reconciliation of memories" with Algeria in order to "calm" (*apaiser*) the relationship between the two countries. In January 2021, the government released a report it commissioned to study France's colonial history in Algeria and recommend a series of measures to address the effects of ongoing historical grievances (relating, for example, to the question of nuclear testing in the Sahara, the repatriation of archives and the cemeteries of Europeans in Algeria). Entitled "France-Algeria: Painful Passions," it was authored by Jewish and Algerian-born historian Benjamin Stora. The document is a strange mix of historiography—covering recent trends in scholarship—and political history, delineating France's official attempts to come to terms with its colonial past over the last two decades. Stora focuses narrowly on the War of Independence (1954–1962), an eight-year conflict whose brutality serves to substantiate his claim about the "singularity" of French Algeria. Echoing a common discourse in France, he presents the colonization of Algeria (condensed in the War of Independence) as incommensurate with other histories of settlement: as an event, rather than a structure. Algeria is also rendered exceptional by an account told through the lens of pathology and emotional attachments. This framing obscures the commonalities between Algeria and California (or Israel) that informed colonial policies.

An example of a common framework that shaped settler-colonial experiences in Israel and French Algeria is the role of religion. In both cases, religion worked as a form of "racial amnesty"—in the sense that Algerian and Israeli Jews fared better than the Muslim inhabitants of these lands.[14] Jews in Algeria received French citizenship in 1870 (something unavailable to Muslims until 1958), and Israel continues to grant citizenship to Jews anywhere in the world. As the scholar Ariella Azoulay has argued, both French and Israeli settlement thus relied on a fabricated "Judeo-Christian tradition," in which Judaism was included in "Western civilization" while Muslims were excluded as foreign.[15]

Stora's report prompted some commentators to write about anti-Jewish sentiment in Algeria without considering the role of Israeli and French government policies in shaping Algerian public opinion. In a recent essay in the *New York Review of Books*, literary critic Alice Kaplan attributes the outcry against the Algerian President Abdelaziz Bouteflika's invitation of the Constantine-born Jewish musician Enrico Macias to visit his native city in 2000 to a resurgence in Algerian antisemitism.[16] Kaplan's analysis overlooks Macias' vocal support for the state of Israel and its military. She also fails to mention that his visit was supported by future French president Nicolas Sarkozy, a close friend who was eager to promote a new initiative for Mediterranean (i.e., European) cooperation with Algeria. Instead of reflecting on how religious identities in both Algeria and Israel have been used to divide Indigenous communities, Kaplan seems to lay the blame squarely on Muslim intolerance. These omissions and inconvenient truths present another example of how ignoring tangled settler-colonial relationships and common structures can lead to a myopic view of the present. Indeed, support for Israel by French Jews has been a reoccurring obstacle to the formation of a united front against Islamophobia and antisemitism in France since the 1980s.

While metropolitan intellectuals close to the state tend to focus on their settler-colonial history as an exception, expressions of Third Wordlist solidarity often take the opposite tack, purposefully highlighting the commonalities among their colonial experiences. For example, during the final match of the 2021 FIFA Arab Cup, Algerian fans chanted "Filastin *shuhada*" in honor of Palestinian "martyrs." Once the final whistle was blown, players ran onto the pitch carrying both Algerian and Palestinian flags. The Algerian media presented the team's success as a victory not only for the Fennecs (as the national team is called) but also for Palestine. One Algerian sports journalist explained the bond between Algeria and Palestine in terms of the fact that "Algerians understand the devastation of settler colonialism."[17] Algerian cartoonists have also drawn parallels between the continued occupation of the Western Sahara by Morocco and Israel's occupation of the Palestinian territories.

Algerians have invoked their own revolutionary legacy to militate for the liberation of Palestine, including during the Hirak, the popular protest movement that began in February 2019. While colonial (and ex-colonial) voices insist on the singularity and exceptionalism of each settler-colonial regime, formerly colonized people embrace the legacy of entanglement and connections to make more radical claims. Depicting settler colonialism as a structure with connections across time and space, rather than an event, continues to be fundamental in fashioning anti-colonial solidarities.

1 Patrick Wolfe, "Settler Colonialism and the Elimination of the Native," *Journal of Genocide Research* 8/4 (December 2006).

2 Benjamin Brower, "Rethinking Abolition in Algeria. Slavery and the 'Indigenous Question'," *Cahiers d'études africaines* 195 (2009).

3 Gerson Shafir, *Land, Labor and the Origins of the Israeli-Palestinian Conflict, 1882–1914* (Cambridge: Cambridge University Press, 1989).

4 Liora R. Halperin, *The Oldest Guard : Forging the Zionist Settler Past* (Stanford: Stanford University Press, 2021).

5 ANOM 81F/2302, Documents Algériens, Série Économique, no. 49, July 15, 1948, "La Culture des Agrumes en Algérie."

6 See Susan Slyomovics, "Who and What is Native to Israel? On Marcel Janco's Settler Art and Jocqueline Shohet Kahanoff's 'Levantinism'," *Settler Colonial Studies* 4/1 (2014).

7 City of Montclair, *Montclair* (Mount Pleasant, CA: Arcadia Publishing, 2005), p. 9.

8 Jared Farmer, *Trees in Paradise: A California History* (New York: W.V. Norton & Company, 2012).

9 Antoine Bernard de Raymond, "Une 'Algérie Californienne'? L'économie politique de la standardisation dans l'Algérie coloniale (1930–1962)," *Politix* 95 (2011), p. 33.

10 Ibid.

11 BNF 8-O2F-1645, École Nationale d'Agriculture d'Alger, "Voyage d'études en Israël de la Promotion 1955-1958," March–April 1958.

12 Shira Robinson, *Citizen Strangers: Palestinians and the Birth of Israel's Liberal Settler State* (Stanford: Stanford University Press, 2013).

13 Eve Tuck and K. Wayne Yang, "Decolonization is not a metaphor," *Decolonization: Indigeneity, Education & Society* 1/1 (2012).

14 Patrick Wolfe, *Traces of History, Elementary Structures of Race* (London and New York: Verso, 2016).

15 Ariella Azoulay, "Algerian Jews Have not Forgotten France's Colonial Crimes," Boston Review, February 10, 2021.

16 Alice Kaplan, "War and Memory in France and Algeria," *New York Review of Books*, November 18, 2021.

17 Linah Alsaafin and Ramy Allahoum, "What is Behind Algeria and Palestine's Footballing Love Affair?" Aljazeera, December 20, 2021.

Women, Land-Struggles and The Valorization of Labor

Silvia Federici

in *The Commoner*,
no. 10 (Spring/Summer 2005)

How can we ever get out of poverty if we can't get a piece of land to work? If we had land to plant, we wouldn't need to get food sent to us all the way from the United States. No. We'd have our own. But as long as the government refuses to give us the land and other resources we need, we'll continue to have foreigners running our country.

Elvia Alvarado (Benjamin 1987:104)

Introduction: Women Keep the World Alive

Until not long ago, issues relating to land and land struggles would have failed to generate much interest among North Americans, unless they were farmers or descendants of the American Indians for whom the importance of land as the foundation of life is still paramount, culturally at least. For the rest of the population, the land question seemed to have receded into a distant past, as in the aftermath of a prolonged urbanization and industrialization process, land no longer appeared as the fundamental means of reproduction, and new technologies claimed to provide the power, self-reliance, and creativity that people once associated with agriculture.

This has been a great loss because this amnesia has led to a world where the basic questions concerning our existence—where our food comes from, whether it nourishes or poisons our bodies—remain unanswered and are often unasked. This indifference to land among urban dwellers is coming to an end, however. Concern for the genetic engineering of agricultural crops and the ecological impact of the destruction of the tropical forests, together with the struggles of indigenous people, like the Zapatistas who have risen up in arms to oppose land privatization, have created a new awareness about the importance of the "land question," not long ago still identified as a "Third World" issue.

There has also been a conceptual shift, in the last twenty years, concerning our understanding of the relation between land and capitalism. This shift has been promoted by the work of activist-scholars like Maria Mies (1986, 1999), Vandana Shiva (1989, 1993), Bennholdt-Thomsen (1999, 2001), and Claudia von Werlhof (2001), who have shown that land is the material basis for women's subsistence work, and the main source of "food security" for millions of people across the planet. Maria Mies also views this subsistence work as the paradigm of a new social perspective, providing a realistic alternative to capitalist globalization.

It is against this political and conceptual background that I examine the struggles that women are making worldwide to gain access to land, boost subsistence farming, and counter the expanding commercialization of natural resources. I argue that these efforts are extremely important. Thanks to them, billions of people are able to survive, and they point in the direction of the changes we have to make if we are to regain control over the means of *production*, and construct a society where our reproduction does not threaten the survival of other people, nor threatens the continuation of life on the planet.

Women and Land: A Historical Perspective

It is an indisputable fact, though one difficult to measure, that women are the subsistence farmers of the planet. That is, women are responsible for and produce the bulk of the food that is consumed by their families (immediate or extended) or that is sold at the local markets for consumption. This is especially true in Africa, even though across the continent women's right to own land is often denied, and women's access to land, in some countries, is possible only through the intervention and mediation of male kin (Wanyeki 2003).[1]

Subsistence farming is difficult to measure because it is unwaged work; thus its status is similar to that of housework. Even the women who are subsistence farmers often do not consider it as work and, despite attempts to measure its significance in quantitative terms, we do not have reliable estimates concerning the number of hours or number of workers involved, and the value of their work.

International agencies like FAO (Food and Agriculture Organization), the ILO (International Labor Organization), and the United Nations have generally overlooked the difficulties posed by the measurement of subsistence work. But they have recognized that much depends on the definition we use. Thus they have noted that:

> In Bangladesh, [the] labour force participation of women was 10 percent according to the Labour Force Survey of 1985/86. But when, in 1989, the Labour Force Survey included in the questionnaire specific activities such as threshing, food-processing and poultry-rearing, the economic activity rate went up to 63 percent (UN 1995:114).[2]

It is not easy, then, on the basis of the few statistics available, to assess how many people, and in particular how many women are involved in subsistence farming; but clearly it is a substantial number. In the case of sub-Saharan Africa, according to FAO (2002), "women produce up to 80 percent of all the basic foodstuffs for household consumption and for sale." Given that the population of sub-Saharan Africa is about three-quarters of a billion people, with a large percentage of children, this means that more than a hundred million African women must be subsistence farmers.[3] Indeed, women hold up *more* than half the sky!

We should also recognize that the persistence of subsistence farming is an astounding phenomenon considering that capitalist development has been premised on the separation of agricultural producers, women above all, from the land. This reality can only be explained on the basis of a tremendous struggle women have made to resist the commercialization of agriculture.

Evidence for this struggle is found throughout the history of colonization, from the Andes to Africa. In response to land expropriation by the Spaniards (assisted by local chiefs), women in Mexico and Peru, in the 16th and 17th centuries, ran to the mountains, rallied the population to resist the foreign invaders, and became the staunchest defenders of the old cultures and religions, which were centered on the worship of nature-gods (Silverblatt 1987; Federici 2004). Later, in the nineteenth century, in Africa and Asia, women defended the traditional female farming systems against the systematic attempts made by the European colonialists to dismantle them and redefine agricultural work as a male job.

As Ester Boserup (among others) has shown, with reference to West Africa, not only did colonial officers, missionaries, and later, agricultural developers impose commercial crops at the expense of food production; though African women did most of the farming, they excluded women from the study of modern farming systems and denied them technical assistance. They also privileged men with regard to land assignment, even when the men were absent from their homes (Boserup 1970:53–55, 59-60). Thus, in addition to eroding women's "traditional" rights as participants in communal land-systems and independent cultivators, the colonialists and developers alike introduced new divisions between women and men. They imposed a new sexual division of labor, based upon women's subordination to men and their confinement to unpaid household labor, which, in the colonialists' schemes, included unpaid cooperation with their husbands in the cultivation of cash-crops.

Women, however, did not accept this deterioration in their social position without protest. In colonial Africa, whenever they feared that the government might sell their land or might appropriate their crops, they revolted. Exemplary is the protest that women mounted against the colonial authorities in Kedjom Keku and Kedjom Ketinguh, in Northwestern (then British) Cameroon, in 1958. Angered by rumors claiming that the government was going to put their land up for sale, 7,000 women repeatedly marched to Bamenda, the provincial capital at the time, and, in their longest stay, camped for two weeks outside the British colonial administrative buildings, "singing loudly and making their rumbustious presence felt" (Diduk 1989:339–340).

In the same region, women fought against the destruction of their subsistence farms by foraging cattle owned by either members of the local male elite or the nomadic Fulani to whom the colonial authorities had granted seasonal pasturage rights expecting to collect a herd tax. In this case too, the women's boisterous protest defeated the plan, forcing the authorities to sanction the offending pastoralists. As Susan Diduk writes,

> In the protests, women perceived themselves as fighting for the survival and subsistence needs of family and kin. Their agricultural labor was and continues to be indispensable to daily food production. Kedjom men also emphasize the importance of these roles in the past and present. Today they are frequently heard to say, "Don't women suffer for farming and for carrying children for nine months? Yes, they do good for the country" (Diduk 1989:343).[4]

There were many similar struggles, in the 1940s and 1950s, throughout Africa, by women resisting the introduction of cash crops, to which the most fertile lands were being allocated, and the extra work it imposed on them, which took them away from their subsistence farming.

How productive women's subsistence farming continued to be, from the viewpoint of the survival of the colonized communities, can be seen from the contribution it made to the anti-colonial struggle and specifically to the maintenance of liberation fighters in the bush (e.g., in Algeria, Kenya, and Mozambique) (Davidson 1981:76–78, 96–8, 170). Similarly, in the post-independence period, women fought against being recruited in agricultural development projects as unpaid "helpers" of their husbands. The best example of this resistance is the intense struggle women made in the Senegambia to refuse to cooperate in the commercial cultivation of rice crops, which came at the expense of their subsistence food production (Carney and Watts 1991).

It is because of these struggles—which are now recognized as the main reason for the failure of agricultural development projects through the 1960s and 1970s (Moser 1993)—that women continue to be the world's main subsistence farmers; and a sizable subsistence sector has survived in many regions of the world, despite the commitment of pre- and post-independence governments to promote "economic development" along capitalist lines. The determination of millions of women in Africa, Asia, and the Americas to not abandon subsistence farming must be emphasized to counter the tendency, present even among radical social scientists, to interpret the survival of subsistence work only as a consequence of international capital's need to cheapen the cost of the reproduction of labor and "liberate" male workers for the cultivation of cash crops and other forms of waged labor.

Claude Meillassoux (1981), the main Marxist proponent of this theory, has argued that female subsistence-oriented production, or the "domestic economy," as he calls it, has ensured a supply of cheap workers for the capitalist sector at home and abroad and, as such, it has subsidized capitalist accumulation. As his argument goes, thanks to the work of the "village," the laborers who migrated to Paris or Johannesburg have provided a "free" commodity to the capitalist who hired them; since the employers did not have to pay for their upbringing nor had to continue to support them with unemployment benefits when their work was no longer needed.

From this perspective, women's labor in subsistence farming would be a bonus for governments, companies, and development agencies, enabling them to more effectively exploit waged workers and transfer wealth from the rural to the urban areas, in effect degrading the quality of the lives of female farmers and their communities (Meillassoux 1981:110–111). To his credit, Meillassoux acknowledges the efforts made by international agencies and governments to "underdevelop" the subsistence sector. He sees the constant draining of its resources and recognizes the precarious nature of this system of labor reproduction, anticipating that it may soon undergo a decisive crisis.[5] But overall, he too has failed to recognize the struggle underpinning the survival of subsistence work and its continuing importance—despite the attacks waged upon it—from the viewpoint of the community's capacity to resist the encroachment of capitalist relations.

As for liberal economists, their view of "subsistence work" degrades it to the level of an "uneconomic," "unproductive" activity (in the same way as liberal economics refuses to see women's unpaid domestic labor in the home as work). As an alternative, liberal economists propose "income generating projects," the universal remedy to poverty in the neo-liberal agenda,[6] and presumably the key to women's emancipation.

What these different perspectives ignore is the strategic importance that access to land and food production has had for women and their communities, despite the ability of companies and governments to use it at times for their own ends. An analogy can be made with the situation that developed during slavery in Jamaica, where the plantation owners gave the slaves small plots of land ("provision grounds") to cultivate for their own support. The owners took this measure to save on food imports and reduce the cost of reproducing their workers. But the slaves were able to take advantage of it, as it gave them more mobility and independence such that—according to some historians—even before emancipation, a proto-peasantry had formed on the island, possessing a remarkable freedom of movement, and already deriving some income from the sale of its own products (Bush 1990; Morrissey 1989).[7]

Extending this analogy to illustrate the post-colonial capitalist use of subsistence labor, we can say that subsistence agriculture has been an important means of support for billions of workers, giving wage laborers the possibility to contract better conditions of work and survive labor strikes and political protests, so that in several countries the wage sector has acquired an importance disproportionate to its small numerical size (Federici 1992).[8]

The "village"—a metaphor for subsistence farming in a communal setting—has been a crucial site also for women's struggle, providing a base from which to reclaim the wealth the state and capital were removing from it. It is a struggle that has taken many forms, often being directed as much against men as against government, but always strengthened by the fact that women had access to land and could also support themselves and their children directly through the production of food and through the sale of their surplus product. Even after becoming urbanized, women have continued to cultivate any patch of land they could gain access to in order to feed their families and maintain a certain degree of autonomy from the market (Bryceson 1993:105–117).

To what extent the village has been a source of power for female and male workers across the former colonial world can be measured by the attack that from the early 1980s through the 1990s the World Bank, the International Monetary Fund (IMF), and the World Trade Organization (WTO) has waged a campaign against it under the guise of Structural Adjustment and "globalization."[9]

The World Bank has made the destruction of subsistence agriculture and the commercialization of land the centerpiece of its ubiquitous structural adjustment programs (Federici 1992; Caffentzis 1995; Faraclas 2001; Turner and Brownhill 2001). As a consequence, large tracts of communal land have been taken over by agribusiness and devoted to export crops, while "cheap" (i.e., subsidized) imported foods from Europe and North America have flooded the liberalized economies of Africa and Asia (which are forbidden to subsidize their farmers), further displacing women farmers from the local markets. War has completed the task, terrorizing millions into flight from their homelands (Federici 2000).

What has followed has been a *reproduction crisis* of proportions not seen even in the colonial period. Even in regions famous for their agricultural productivity, like southern Nigeria, food is now scarce or too expensive to be within reach of the average person who, after the implementation of structural adjustment programs, has to contend simultaneously with price hikes, frozen wages, devalued currency, widespread unemployment, and cuts in social services.[10]

This is where the importance of women's struggles for land stands out. Women have been the main buffer for the world proletariat against starvation imposed by the World Bank's neo-liberal regime. They have been the main opponents of the neo-liberal demand that "market prices" determine who should live and who should die, and they are the ones who have provided a practical model for the reproduction of life in a non-capitalist way.

Struggles for Subsistence and Against "Globalization" in Africa, Asia, and the Americas

Faced with a renewed drive toward land privatization, the extension of cash crops, and the rise in food prices due to economic adjustment and globalization, women have resorted to many strategies to continue to support their families, pitting them against the most powerful institutions on the planet.

One of the primary strategies women have adopted to defend their communities from the impact of economic adjustment and dependence on the global market has been the expansion of subsistence farming also in the urban centers.

Exemplary is the case of Guinea Bissau studied by Galli and Funk (1995), which shows that, since the early 1980s, women have planted small gardens with vegetables, cassava, and fruit trees around most houses in the capital city of Bissau and other towns; and in times of scarcity, they have preferred to forfeit the earnings they might have made selling their produce to ensure their families would not go without food.[11] Still with reference to Africa, this picture is confirmed by Christa Wichterich, who describes women subsistence farming and urban gardening as "cooking pot economics." She too notes that in the 1990s, it was revived in many African cities; the urban farmers being mostly women from the lower class:

> There were onions and papaya trees, instead of flower borders, in front of the housing estates of underpaid civil servants in Dar-es-Salaam; chickens and banana plants in the backyards of Lusaka; vegetables on the wide central reservations of the arterial roads of Kampala, and especially of Kinshasa, where the food supply system had largely collapsed... In [Kenyan] towns [too]...green roadside strips, front gardens and wasteland sites were immediately occupied with maize, plants, *sukum wiki*, the most popular type of cabbage. (Wichterich 2000:73)

However, in order to expand food production, women have had to battle to expand their access to land, which the international agencies' drives to privatize land and commercialize agriculture have further jeopardized.

This may be the reason why, in the case of Guinea Bissau, many women have chosen to remain in the rural area, while most of the men have migrated, resulting in a "feminization of the rural areas," with many villages now consisting of women farming alone or in women's coops (Galli and Funk 1995:23).

Regaining or expanding land for subsistence farming has been one of the main battles also for rural women in Bangladesh, leading to the formation of the Landless Women Association that has been carrying on land occupations since 1992. During this period, the Association has managed to settle 50,000 families, often confronting landowners in pitched confrontations. According to Shamsun Nahar Khan Doli, a leader of the Association to whom I owe this report, many occupations are on "chars," low-lying islands formed by soil deposits in the middle of a river.[12] Such new lands should be allocated to landless farmers, according to Bangladeshi law, but because of the growing commercial value of land, big landowners have increasingly seized them. Women are now organizing to stop them, defending themselves with brooms, spears of bamboo, and even knives. Women have also set up alarm systems to gather other women when boats with the landowners or their goons approach, and push the attackers off or stop them from landing.

Similar land struggles are being fought in South America. In Paraguay, for example, the Peasant Women's Commission (CMC) was formed in 1985 in alliance with the Paraguayan Peasant's Movement (MCP) to demand land distribution (Fisher 1993:86). As Jo Fischer points out, the CMC was the first peasant women's movement that went into the streets in support of its demands, and incorporated in its program women's concerns, also condemning "their double oppression, both as peasants and as women" (Fisher 1993:87).

The turning point for the CMC came when the government granted large tracts of land to the peasant movement in the forests close to the Brazilian border. The women took these grants as an opportunity to organize a model community, joining together to collectively farm their strips of land. As Geraldina, an early founder of CMC, pointed out,

> We work all the time, more now than ever before, but we've also changed the way we work. We're experimenting with communal work to see if it gives us more time for other things. It also gives us a chance to share our experiences and worries. This is a very different way of living for us. Before, we didn't even know our neighbors. (Fisher 1993:98).

Women's land struggles have included the defense of communities threatened by commercial housing projects constructed in the name of "urban development." "Housing" has often involved the loss of "land" for food production historically. An example is the struggle of women in the Kawaala neighborhood of Kampala (Uganda), where the World Bank, in conjunction with the Kampala City Council (KCC), in 1992–1993, sponsored a large housing project that would destroy much subsistence farmland around or near people's homes. Not surprisingly, it was women who most strenuously organized against it, through the formation of an Abataka (Residents) Committee, eventually forcing the Bank to withdraw from the project. According to one of the women leaders:

> While men were shying away, women were able to say anything in public meetings in front of government officials. Women were more vocal because they were directly affected. It is very hard for women to stand without any means of income....most of these women are people who basically support their children, and without any income and food, they cannot do it. You come and take their peace and income, and they are going to fight, not because they want to, but because they have been oppressed and suppressed. (Tripp 2000:183)

Aili Mari Tripp points out that the situation in the Kawaala neighborhood is far from unique.[13] Similar struggles have been reported from different parts of Africa and Asia, where peasant women's organizations have opposed the development of industrial zones threatening to displace them and their families and contaminate the environment.

Industrial or commercial housing development often clashes, today, with women's subsistence farming, in a context in which more and more women even in urban centers, are gardening (in Kampala women grow 45 percent of the food for their families). It is important to add that in defending land from assault by commercial interests and affirming the principle that "land and life are not for sale," women again, as in the past against colonial invasion, are defending their people's history and their culture. In the case of Kawaala, the majority of residents on the disputed land had been living there for generations and had buried their kin there—for many in Uganda the ultimate evidence of land ownership. Tripp's reflections on this land struggle are pertinent to my thesis:

> Stepping back from the events of the conflict, it becomes evident that the residents, especially the women involved, were trying to institutionalize some new norms for community mobilization, not just in Kawaala but more widely in providing a model for other community projects. They had a vision of a

> more collaborative effort that took the needs of women, widows, children, and the elderly as a starting point and recognized their dependence on the land for survival. (Tripp 2000:194)

Two more developments need to be mentioned in conjunction with women's defense of subsistence production. First, there has been the formation of regional systems of self-sufficiency aiming to guarantee "food security" and maintain an economy based on solidarity and the refusal of competition. The most impressive example in this respect comes from India where women formed the National Alliance for Women's Food Rights, a national movement made of thirty-five women's groups. One of the main efforts of the Alliance has been the campaign in defense of the mustard seed economy that is crucial for many rural and urban women in India. A subsistence crop, the seed has been threatened by the attempts of multinational corporations based in the United States to impose genetically-engineered soybeans as a source of cooking oil.[14] In response, the Alliance has built "direct producer-consumer alliances" to "defend the livelihood of farmers and the diverse cultural choices of consumers," as stated by Vandana Shiva (2000), one of the leaders of the movement. In her words: "We protest soybean imports and call for a ban on the import of genetically-engineered soybean products. As the women from the slums of Delhi sing, 'Sarson Bachao, Soya Bhagaa,' or, 'Save the Mustard, Dump the Soya'" (Shiva 2000).

Second, across the world, women have been leading the struggle to prevent commercial logging and save or rebuild forests, which are the foundation of people's subsistence economies, providing nourishment as well as fuel, medicine, and communal relations. Forests, Shiva writes, echoing testimonies coming from every part of the planet, are "the highest expression of earth's fertility and productivity" (Shiva 1989:56). Thus, when forests come under assault it is a death sentence for the tribal people who live in them, especially the women. Therefore, women do everything to stop the loggers. Shiva often cites, in this context, the Chipko movement—a movement of women in Garhwal, in the foothills of the Himalayas who, beginning in the early 1970s, embrace the trees destined to fall and put their bodies between them and the saws when the loggers come (Shiva 1989).

While women in Garhwal have mobilized to prevent forests from being cut down, in villages of Northern Thailand they have protested the Eucalyptus plantations forcibly planted on their expropriated farms by a Japanese paper-making company with the support of the Thai military government (Matsui 1996:88–90). In Africa, an important initiative has been the "Green Belt Movement," which under the leadership of Wangari Maathai is committed to planting a green belt around the major cities and, since 1977, has planted tens of millions of trees to prevent deforestation, soil loss, desertification, and fuel-wood scarcity (Maathai 1993).

But the most striking struggle for the survival of the forests is taking place in the Niger Delta, where the mangrove tree swamps are being threatened by oil production. Opposition to it has mounted for twenty years, beginning in Ogharefe, in 1984, when several thousand women from the area laid siege to Pan Ocean's Production Station demanding compensation for the destruction of the water, trees, and land. To show their determination, the women also threatened to disrobe should their demands be frustrated—a threat they put into action when the company's director arrived, so that he found himself surrounded by thousands of women naked, a serious curse in the eyes of the Niger Delta communities, which convinced him at the time to accept the reparation claims (Turner and Oshare 1994:140–141).

The struggle over land has also grown since the 1970s in the most unlikely place—New York City—in the form of an urban gardening movement. It began with the initiative of a women-led group called the "Green Guerrillas," who began cleaning up vacant lots in the Lower East Side. By the 1990s, eight hundred and fifty urban gardens had developed in the city and dozens of community coalitions had formed, such as the Greening of Harlem Coalition that was begun by a group of women who wanted "to reconnect with the earth and give children an alternative to the streets." Now it counts more than twenty-one organizations and thirty garden projects (Wilson and Weinberg 1999:36).

It is important to note here that the gardens have been not only a source of vegetables and flowers, but have served community-building and have been a stepping stone for other community struggles (like squatting and homesteading). Because of this work, the women came under attack during Mayor Giuliani's regime, and for some years now one of the main challenges this movement has faced has been stopping the bulldozers. Over the last decade, a hundred gardens have been lost to "development," more than forty have been slated for bulldozing, and the prospects for the future seem gloomy (Wilson and Weinberg 1999:61). Since his appointment, in fact, the mayor of New York City, Michael Bloomberg, like his predecessor, has declared war on these gardens.

The Importance of the Struggle

As we have seen, in cities across the world at least a quarter of the people depend on food produced by women's subsistence labor. In Africa, for example, a quarter of the people living in towns say they could not survive without subsistence food production. This is confirmed by the UN Population Fund which claims that "some two hundred million city dwellers are growing food, providing about one billion people with at least part of their food supply" (UN 2001). When we consider that the bulk of the food subsistence producers are women, we can see why the men of Kedjom, Cameroon would say, "Yes, women subsistence farmers do good for humanity." Thanks to them, the billions of people, rural and urban, who earn one or two dollars a day do not go under, even in times of economic crisis.

Equally important, women's subsistence production counters the trend by agribusiness to reduce cropland—one of the causes of high food prices and starvation—while ensuring control over the quality of food and protecting consumers against manipulation of crops and poisoning by pesticides. Further, women's subsistence production represents a safe way of farming, a crucial consideration at a time when the effects of pesticides on agricultural crops are causing high rates of mortality and disease among peasants across the world, starting with women (see, for example, Settimi et al. 1999). Thus, subsistence farming gives women an essential means of control over their health and the health and lives of their families (Bennholdt-Thomsen and Mies 1999).

Most importantly, we can also see that subsistence production is contributing to a non-competitive, solidarity-centered mode of life that is crucial for the building of a new society. It is the seed of what Veronika Bennholdt-Thomsen and Maria Mies call the "other" economy which "puts life and everything necessary to produce and maintain life on this planet at the center of economic and social activity and not the never-ending accumulation of dead money" (Bennholdt-Thomsen and Mies 1999:5).

1 A detailed description of the land tenure system and women's property rights in seven African countries—Cameroon, Ethiopia, Mozambique, Nigeria, Rwanda, Senegal, Uganda—is found in *Women and Land in Africa* (2003) by Muthoni L. Wanyeki. The author found that in general women control food crop production (in some countries like Uganda up to 90%) and control the benefits resulting from the sale of surplus crops. However, their right to own and inherit land is generally limited or denied, especially in patrilineal cultures. African women have access to land according to customary laws, but they have users' rights through their relations with men, through marriage or inheritance. In Latin America as well, women's land ownership rights have been extremely restricted, by means of "legal, cultural, and institutional" mechanisms rooted in a patriarchal ideology and patriarchal division of labor. On this subject see Deere and Leon (2001) pp. 2–3.

2 In 1988, the ILO defined subsistence workers in agriculture and fishing as those who "provide food, shelter and a minimum of cash income for themselves and their households" (UN 1995:114)—a fuzzy definition depending on which notion of "minimum cash income" and "provision" one uses. Moreover, its operative meaning is derived from intentions, e.g., the subsistence workers' lack of "market orientation," and deficiencies they experience, such as having no access to formal credit and advanced technology.

3 The social and economic impact of colonialism varied greatly, depending (in part) on the duration of direct colonial control. We may even interpret the present differences in women's participation in subsistence and cash-crop agriculture as a measure of the extent of colonial appropriation of land. Using the UN-ILO labor force participation statistics, and remembering the measurement problem concerning subsistence farming, we see that sub-Saharan Africa has the highest percentage of the female labor force in agriculture (75 percent); while in Southern Asia it is 55 percent; South-East Asia, 42 percent; and East Asia, 35 percent. By contrast, South and Central America have low women's participation rates in agriculture similar to those found in "developed" regions like Europe, between 7 and 10 percent. That is, the participation rates roughly correlate with the duration of formal colonialism in the regions.

4 On the struggles of women farmers in western Cameroon in the 1950s, see also Margaret Snyder and Mary Tadesse, who write: "Women continued to persist in their economic activities during colonial times, despite the formidable odds they faced. One example is the way they mobilized to form corn mill societies in western Cameroon in the 1950s. Over time, 200 such societies were formed with a total membership of 18,000. They used grinding mills that were owned in common, fenced their fields, and constructed water storage units and co-operative stores... In other words, 'for generations, women established some form of collective actions to increase group productivity, to fill-in socio-economic gaps wherever the colonial administration failed, or to protest policies that deprived them of the resources to provide for their families.'" (Snyder and Tadesse 1995:23).

5 The crisis consists in the fact that if the domestic economy becomes too unproductive, it then fails to reproduce the immigrant worker, but if it becomes too productive, it drives up the costs of labor, as the worker in this case can avoid wage labor.

6 Exemplary here is Caroline Moser, a "World Bank feminist," who executes a very sophisticated analysis of the work of women and whose approach to women is, in her terms, "emancipatory." After presenting a careful analysis of the many theoretical approaches to women's labor (Marxist included), the case studies she examines are two "income generating" projects and a "food for work" scheme (Moser 1993:235–238).

7 However, as soon as the price of sugar on the world market went up, the plantation owner cut the time allotted to the slave for cultivation of their provision grounds.

8 See, e.g., what Michael Chege (1987:250) writes of African wage workers and the land: "...most African laborers maintain a foothold in the countryside; the existence of labor totally alienated from land ownership is yet to happen." One of the consequences of this "lack of alienation" is that the African worker can rely on a material basis of solidarity (especially the provision of food) from the village whenever s/he decides to strike.

9 The attack waged by the World Bank through Structural Adjustment *falsifies* Meillassoux's claim that the domestic economy is functional to capitalism, but *verifies* his prediction that a "final" crisis of capitalism looms because of its inability to preserve and control the domestic economy (Meillassoux 1981:141).

10 Witness the dramatic decline in the "real wage" and the increase in the rate of poverty in Nigeria. Once considered a "middle income" country, Nigeria now has 70 percent of its population living on less than one U.S. dollar a day, and 90 percent on less than two U.S. dollars a day (cf., UN Development Program statistics from its website).

11 In Bissau, women planted rice during the rainy season in plots on the peripheries of town. During the dry season, more enterprising women try to get access to nearby plots in order to plant irrigated vegetables not only for domestic consumption but for sale (Galli and Funk 1995:20).

12 This report is based on an oral testimony at the Prague "Countersummit" of 2000.

13 Tripp concludes that "... the Kawaala struggle is in many ways a microcosm of some of the changes that are occurring in Uganda" (Tripp 2000:194). Similar struggles have been waged throughout the Third World, where peasant women's organizations have opposed the development of industrial zones threatening to displace them and their families and contaminate the environment.

14 This attempt was given a boost in 1998 when the mustard seed cooking oil, locally produced and distributed, was mysteriously found to be adulterated to such a point that forty-one people died after consuming it. The government then banned its production and sale. The National Alliance responded by taking the case to court and calling on producers and consumers not to cooperate with the government's ban (Shiva 2000:54).

References

Benjamin, Medea, ed. 1987. *Don't Be Afraid Gringo: A Honduran Woman Speaks from the Heart: The Story of Elvia Alvarado*. New York: HarperPerennial.

Bennholdt-Thomsen, Veronika, **Nicholas Faraclas**, and **Claudia von Werlhof**, eds. 2001. *There is an Alternative: Subsistence and Worldwide Resistance to Corporate Globalization*. London: Zed.

Bennholdt-Thomsen, Veronika and **Maria Mies**. 1999. *The Subsistence Perspective: Beyond the Globalised Economy*. London: Zed.

Boserup, Ester. 1970. *Women's Role in Economic Development*. London: George Allen and Unwin Ltd.

Bryceson, Deborah Fahy. 1993. *Liberalizing Tanzania's Food Trade. Private and Public Faces of Urba Marketing Policy. 1930–1988*. London: Zed Books.

Bush, Barbara. 1990. *Slave Women in Caribbean Society, 1650-1838*. Bloomington, IN: Indiana University Press.

Caffentzis, George. 1995. "The fundamental implications of the Debt Crisis for social reproduction in Africa." In *Paying the Price: Women and the Politics of International Economic Strategy*, edited by M. Dalla Costa and G.F. Dalla Costa. London: Zed Books.

Carney, Judith and **Watts, Michael**. 1991. "Disciplining Women? Rice, Mechanization, and the Evolution of Mandinka Gender Relations in Senegambia." *Signs* 16(4): 651–681.

Chege, Michael. 1987. "The State and Labour in Kenya," In *Popular Struggles for Democracy in Africa*, edited by Peter Anyang' Nyong'o. London: Zed Books.

Davidson, Basil. 1981. *The People's Cause: A History of Guerillas in Africa*. London: Longman.

Deere, Carmen Diana and **Magdalena Léon**. 2001. *Empowering Women. Land and Property Rights in Latin America*. Pittsburgh: University of Pittsburgh.

Diduk, Susan. 1989. "Women's Agricultural Production and Political Action in the Cameroon Grassfields." *Africa* 59(3): 338–355.

FAO. 2002. *Gender and Agriculture*. Retrieved March 18, 2002. http://www.fao.org/Gender/agrib4-e.htm

Faraclas, Nicholas. 2001. "Melanesia, the Banks, and the BINGOs: Real Alternatives are Everywhere (Except in the Consultants' Briefcases)." In *There is an Alternative: Subsistence and Worldwide Resistance to Corporate Globalization*, edited by Veronika Bennholdt-Thomsen, Nicholas Faraclas, and Claudia von Werlhof. London: Zed.

Federici, Silvia. 1992. "The Debt Crisis, Africa, and the New Enclosures." In *Midnight Oil: Work, Energy, War, 1973–1992*, edited by Midnight Notes. New York: Autonomedia.

—. "Reproduction and Feminist Struggle in the New International Division of Labor." In *Women, Development and Labor of Reproduction: Struggles and Movements*, edited by M. Dalla Costa and G. F. Dalla Costa. Trenton, NJ: Africa World Press.

—. *Caliban and the Witch: Women, the Body, and Primitive Accumulation*. Brooklyn, NY: Autonomedia.

Fisher, Jo. 1993. *Out of the Shadows: Women, Resistance and Politics in South America*. London: Latin American Bureau.

Galli, Rosemary and **Ursula Frank**. 1995. "Structural Adjustment and Gender in Guinea Bissau." In *Women Pay the Price: Structural Adjustment in Africa and the Caribbean*, edited by Gloria T. Emeagwali. NJ: Africa World Press.

Maathai, Wangari. 1993. "Kenya's Green Belt Movement." In *Africa*, Fifth Edition, edited by F. Jeffress Ramsay. Guilford, CT: The Dushkin Publishing Group.

Matsui, Yayori. 1996. *Women in the New Asia: From Pain to Power*. London: Zed Books.

Meillassoux, Claude. 1981. *Maidens, Meal and Money: Capitalism and the Domestic Community*. Cambridge: Cambridge University Press.

Mies, Maria. 1986. *Patriarchy and Accumulation on a World Scale: Women in the International Division of Labour*. London: Zed Books.

Mies, Maria and **Vandana Shiva**. 1993. *Ecofeminism*. London: Zed.

Morrisey, Marietta. 1989. *Slave Women in the New World*. Lawrence: University Press of Kansas.

Moser, Caroline O. N. 1993. *Gender Planning and Development: Theory, Practice and Training*. London: Routledge.

Scott, James C. 1985. *Weapons of the Weak: Everyday Forms of Peasant Resistance*. New Haven: Yale University Press.

Settimi, L. et al. 1999. "Cancer Risk Among Female Agricultural Workers: A Multi-Center Case-Control Study." *American Journal of Industrial Medicine* 36:135-141.

Shiva, Vandana. 1989. *Staying Alive: Women, Ecology and Development*. London: Zed Books.

—. 2000. *Stolen Harvest: Hijacking of the Global Food Supply*. Boston: South End Press.

Silverblatt, Irene. 1987. *Moon, Sun, and Witches: Gender Ideologies and Class in Inca and Colonial Peru*. Princeton: Princeton University Press.

Tripp, Aili Mari. 2000. *Women and Politics in Uganda*. Oxford: James Currey.

Turner, Terisa E. and **Leigh S. Brownhill**, eds. 2001a. *Gender, Feminism and the Civil Commons. A Special Issue of Canadian Journal of Development Studies*. Volume XXII.

—. 2001b. "African Jubilee: Mau Mau Resurgence and the Fight for Fertility in Kenya, 1986–2001." In *Gender, Feminism and the Civil Commons. A Special Issue of Canadian Journal of Development Studies* Volume XXII, edited by Terisa E. Turner and Leigh S. Brownhill.

Turner, Terisa E. and **M.O. Oshare**. 1994. "Women's Uprisings Against the Nigerian Oil Industry." In *Arise! Ye Mighty People!: Gender, Class and Race in Popular Struggles*, edited by Terisa Turner. Trenton: Africa World Press.

United Nations. 1995. *The World's Women 1995: Trends and Statistics*. New York: UN.

United Nations Population Fund. 2001. *State of the World Population 2001*. New York: UN.

Wanyeki, Muthoni L. 2003. *Women and Land in Africa. Culture, Religion and Realizing Women's Rights*. London: Zed Books.

Wichterich, Christa. 2000. *The Globalized Woman: Reports from a Future of Inequality*. London: Zed.

Wilson, Peter Lamborn and **Bill Weinberg**. 1999. *Avantgardening. Ecological Struggles in the City and the World*. New York: Autonomedia.

Race, real estate and real abstraction

Brenna Bhandar and Alberto Toscano

in *Radical Philosophy*,
no. 194 (November 1, 2015).

The crises and mutations of contemporary capitalism have rendered palpable Marx's observation according to which in bourgeois modernity human beings are 'ruled by abstractions'.[1] The processes of financialization animating the dynamics of the 2007–8 crisis involved the violent irruption into the everyday lives of millions of a panoply of ominous acronyms (ABSs, CDOs, SIVs, HFT, and so on), indices of highly mathematized strategies of profit extraction whose mechanics were often opaque to their own beneficiaries. At the same time, this process of financialization was articulated to the most seemingly 'concrete', 'tangible' and thus desirable use and exchange value available to the citizens of so-called advanced liberal democracies: the home. This is a site, a social relation, that as Ferreira da Silva and Chakravartty have noted encompasses the 'juridical, political and economic', thus serving as a lived material synthesis of the three main axes of modern thought.[2]

In the United States, it was quickly revealed – indeed, it had been pointed out before the crisis by some critical geographers[3] – that the devastating socialization of the costs of accumulation via the housing market took deeply racialized (and gendered) forms, grafting, through a host of complex mediations, the forbiddingly impersonal realities of derivative contracts onto the deep and ongoing racial history of property markets and urban geographies. In this article, we want to think through this articulation of race, property and capitalist abstraction, exploring how attention to the forms of property may permit novel and politically urgent insights into the relationship between capitalism and race, addressing a critical area of social contestation in which processes of racialization are intensely present, but in which they are also frequently 'disappeared'.[4] We revisit the place of property in Marxist theories of abstraction, to consider whether it can provide us with some of the instruments to think the present conjuncture, but also to explore the ways in which a consideration of the racial logics of property may require us to recalibrate our understanding of the violence of abstraction.

Separation, dissolution, abstraction

If we take Marx to have been engaged in the practical, emancipatory critique of capitalism, not just as a class system of exploitation but as a social form of abstract domination, then we can understand that under the misleadingly simple slogan 'the abolition of private property' lies the formidable problem of transcending a social relation, 'bourgeois property', which serves as the crucial nexus between the state (the object of Marx's earliest critique) and the economy. In what sense is the question of private property a question of abstraction? Above all, perhaps, in the sense that private property (understood not as personal possession but as the legally sanctioned power to dispose of the means of production, and thus to dispose of labour-power: property as synonymous with capital) depends on a social process of *separation* – abstraction in the etymological sense of pulling out, extracting. In one of Marx's most important mature treatments of the question of property, the section on pre-capitalist formations in the notebooks later collected as the *Grundrisse*, this separation is discussed in terms of a *dissolution*.

In passages that foreshadow his treatment of so-called primitive accumulation in the first volume of *Capital*, Marx depicts capitalism as the first system in which political or communal relations are no longer presupposed by property but are 'posed' by it. Far from being conditioned by a pre-existing community, property qua capital becomes the only real community, the one dominated by abstraction, by money. As he writes, 'the relation of labour to capital ... presupposes a process of history which dissolves the various forms in which the worker is a proprietor, or in which the proprietor works.' He is alluding to the dissolution of the relation to the earth, in which there is 'direct common property';[5] the dissolution of proprietorship of the instrument (in craft production); the dissolution of the means of subsistence; and the dissolution of serfdom and slavery. These are the 'historic presuppositions' 'needed before the worker can be found as a free worker, as objectless, purely subjective labour capacity confronting the objective conditions of production as his *not-property*, as *alien property*, as *value* for-itself, as capital.'[6] This process, which Marx strikingly terms that of 'dissolution into capital', is one in which 'The objective conditions of labour now confront these unbound, propertyless individuals only in the form of values, self-sufficient values.'[7] 'Private property' is thus understood as a double movement of abstraction, one that is conditioned by historical processes of separation but which in its real subsumption of social life continues to serve as a potent agent of dissolution.

This theme of dissolution was already present in Marx's thinking about the political and economic functions of *landed* property back in the *Economic and Philosophical Manuscripts*, where he wrote: 'It is necessary that this appearance be abolished – that landed property, the root of private property, be dragged completely into the movement of private property and that it become a commodity; that the rule of the proprietor appear as the undisguised rule of private property, of capital, freed of all political tincture.'[8] For the purposes of our argument, we should be sensitive to the different accents given in Marx's early and later work to this theme of property as the dissolution (which is to say the abstraction) of social bonds. Roughly, property is presented in the early Marx's work as an agent of abstraction whose real subsumption of social life (and destruction of concrete community) serves as a kind of tragic but necessary prelude to emancipation, to the emergence of a universality antagonistic to that of capital. In the *Grundrisse*, we can instead discern a way of thinking both the rupture represented by the emergence of capitalist property and the persistence (albeit overdetermined by capitalist forms) of so-called pre-capitalist relations. This is what the Hegelian formulation – property now posing its own presuppositions – entails. (It is also, as we shall discuss below, what Stuart Hall was trying to capture in his deployment of the Althusserian notion of *articulation*.)

In his *Intellectual and Manual Labour*, elaborating on Marx's insights into the commodity form, the German philosopher Alfred Sohn-Rethel argued that the origins of the abstract concepts of ancient philosophy were to be located in what he called 'the exchange-abstraction', the activity of generalized commodity-exchange and monetization that served as the unconscious practical 'social synthesis' of Ancient Greek society. It was the existence of a *really abstract social practice* which stood as the presupposition of mental or intellectual abstraction. It was because the Ancient Greeks acted abstractly, so to speak, that they could think abstractly. Marx's uniqueness for Sohn-Rethel lay in being able to provide the means for fully historical, practical explanations of the emergence of seemingly ahistorical forms. Applying Marx's understanding of the commodity to the study of the social unconscious of philosophy allowed one to see how the practice of exchange served as the concrete spatio-temporal basis for a thinking that could powerfully abstract from both space and time. To paraphrase Sohn-Rethel: abstraction is therefore the effect of the action of men, and not of their thought. In reality, it takes place 'behind their backs', at the blind spot, so to speak, of human consciousness.[9] That is where the thinking and efforts of men are absorbed by their acts of exchange.

Now, in what sense can we treat property (more accurately: the legal forms of private property) as a 'real abstraction'? However we may frame or interpret it, there is a prima facie force to the notion that the imposition and generalization of private property did (and continue to) play a formidable role in dissolving social and communal relations, or at the very least in 'positing' them as internal to a property logic. Private property's role as an agent of separation from means of production and subsistence is also not in doubt, and lies at the centre of a vibrant contemporary debate on the 'commons' and 'common goods'.[10] Yet a key feature of the account of real abstraction in Sohn-Rethel, arguably present in certain formulations of Marx also, is troubled by greater attention to the *legal* forms of property. That feature is the *unconscious* character ascribed to commodity-exchange as a form of practical abstraction. Any account of the pre-capitalist presuppositions of capitalist abstract domination cannot rest content, as Sohn-Rethel seems to, with investigating the exchange-abstraction in ancient forms of commodity-based socialization. It also requires thinking of the specificity of legal abstractions as deliberate devices of social organization which were in turn necessary but not sufficient presuppositions for the emergence of capitalism.

The legal historian Yan Thomas, writing on Roman law, suggests we should think of abstraction as constitutive of the operations of the law. This is true of the 'formal *dispositif* that isolates in each of us, abstracting from what is irreducibly singular in us, a juridical personality, in which almost nothing appears of our physical, psychic and social reality, because it is reduced to a single function: our capacity to hold and exercise rights.'[11] Here we can see how modern law is conceived in terms of a twofold process 'of incarnation and naturalization, on the one hand, and of separation and abstraction, on the other, of the juridical person'.[12] It is also at work, importantly, in what Thomas presents as the 'juridical constitution of things in general',[13] where the *res* stands both for appropriable things of property and commerce, on the one hand, and sacred or public inappropriable things, *res nullius in bonis*, on the other.[14] Thomas presents his 'proceduralist' approach as one that can reveal how Roman law 'already had a formalist and abstract idea of the economy' (by contrast with what has been argued by the historical anthropology of the ancient world); for him, 'the history of law partakes of a history of the techniques and instruments through which the putting into abstract form of our societies has taken place.' If that is not properly grasped, he warns, 'the singularity of that history and the specificity of its object' will be totally missed. Thomas shows how the reduction of a thing (*res*) to its price (*pretium*) – the identity of being and value, in other words – was itself a product of juridical procedure, or legal judgment, in which the *res* was 'abstracted and reduced to its value', permitting a 'representation of a purely countable substance of goods',[15] in its turn made possible by the circumscription of a sacred or public sphere of unappropriable goods. In Michele Spanò's gloss, 'law – the most efficacious speech – has a power of transformation without equals: it is a machine for abstraction which, through the medium of language, translates the real and produces it otherwise.'[16]

In light of the Marxist debate surveyed here, the question arises: what is the relation between the social practices of abstraction (grounded in abstract labour and the commodity form) that Marx and Marxists have posited as somehow 'beneath' or 'before' the juridical, though articulated with it, and even requiring it as an 'indispensable moment', and what Thomas calls 'the political construction of the commodity'[17] by law, which would appear to present the operation of abstraction as a deliberate juridical procedure, conditioning economic valorization and accumulation, rather than the other way around? Answering such questions might also require at least posing the problem of the extent to which private property as a moment of capital and private property in property law are superimposable without remainder.

Property between law and capital

In 1865, Marx wrote this about Proudhon:

> Thus history itself had expressed its criticism upon past *property relations*. What Proudhon was actually dealing with was *modern bourgeois property* as it exists today. The question of what this is could have only been answered by a critical analysis of '*political economy*', embracing the totality of these *property relations*, considering not their *legal* aspect as *relations of volition* but their real form, that is, as *relations of production*.[18]

In this passage is encapsulated what would become, especially in the 1960s and 1970s, a vexed question within Marxist debates about law, debates which were in many ways motivated by the now largely forgotten debates about the forms of property and the transition to socialism, but which were perhaps most memorably encapsulated in E.P. Thompson's much-quoted acerbic retort to Althusser that in the history of English capitalism law was to be found 'at every bloody level'. Without trying to summarize these debates we can note that Marx himself stayed true to his observation, made as early as 1847 in 'Moralizing Criticism and Critical Morality', that 'private property is not an abstract concept or a simple relation but the totality of bourgeois relations of production'[19] and thus that treating private property as synonymous with its purely legal form or that form's conceptual and ahistorical hypostasis was insufficient.

Whence the various attempts to distinguish, in ways which at times seem to re-propose the old distinction between (real) possession and (legal) property, between property as legally inscribed and property as a social relation that may exceed its legal form.[20] Thus Nicos Poulantzas would write of how he and Charles Bettelheim had 'noted that it is necessary to distinguish, in the term "property" used by Marx, formal legal property, which may not belong to the 'individual' capitalist, and economic property or real appropriation, which is the only genuine economic power'.[21] In *Reading Capital*, Étienne Balibar notes that for Marx juridical forms are supremely ambivalent, as they 'express' and 'codify' at the same time as they mask economic reality. More importantly for our purposes, though he recognizes the need to keep the space between law, politics and economy open, he also observes how in the specific case of property. This is rendered terminologically and conceptually arduous:

> Hence a difficult *terminological* problem as well, since the concepts in which the relations of production are expressed are precisely concepts in which the economic and the legal are indistinct, starting with the concept of *property*. What is 'property' insofar as it forms a system within the relatively autonomous structure of production, and logically precedes the law of property peculiar to the society considered? Such is the problem which must be initiated for capitalism *too*.[22]

Every element in the mode of production under capitalism is said by Balibar, then, to receive a 'juridical qualification'; it is inscribed in a legal system marked by its abstract universality, a universality which is a reflection of the commodity system – such that the commodity would serve as the cell-form for social abstraction under capitalism.[23] Criticizing Bettelheim's notion of 'economic property' in a later text, Balibar would go further and note that the risk in such a notion (aside from introducing the law of property into a concept whose purpose was to keep it at a distance) was that while rightly not wishing to confuse relations of production and juridical forms of property, it neglected the practical historical role of juridical forms of property, the fact that juridical form was an indispensable moment in capital accumulation; that the accumulation and concentration of capital 'cannot take place without a systematic use of the resources of property law'.[24]

This bears some relation to the critique rendered by Paul Hirst of the place of property in the Marxist legal theories of Evgeny Pashukanis and Karl Renner. Hirst criticizes Marxist theories of the law that reduce legal subjectivity down to the archetypical capitalist, the subject of property right, who engages in economic calculation.[25] The joint-stock company and the shareholder, Hirst argued, represents a type of ownership that is not confined by the 'triple coincidence of property, possession and calculation [in exchange]' that lies at the heart of Marxist considerations of property law. Moreover, the problem of what 'capital' is cannot be separated from questions of the legal definition of its form of organization. As the emergence of the joint-stock company illustrates, 'there is no given form of this organization'.[26] In other words, inventiveness, and a certain amount of flexibility in legal forms, enabling the emergence of new configurations of ownership and market relations, may be as central to our understanding of property as a juridical, economic and social relation as are laws which are taken to directly express the commodity form in its fundamental coordinates.

Articulating race and property

In light of the aforementioned discussions, we can say that to understand the *abstractive powers* of property law – and their articulation with and use of racial difference in processes of propertization and profit – we cannot simply treat property forms as reflections or adjuncts of commodity forms, which is also to say that we cannot treat the question of the practical reality of abstraction as one which is simply adjudicated at the (very abstract) level of the formal analysis of capital. What we would seem to require is a way of thinking the *articulation* between distinct and sometimes independent modalities of abstraction. We would need to be able to think the articulation between *events* and *processes* of abstraction/dissolution (the moments of primitive accumulation or accumulation by dispossession); the 'unconscious' abstracting social *practices* (as grasped, for instance, in Sohn-Rethel's account of the exchange-abstraction); the high-level *logic* of abstraction intrinsic to value as a social form of capitalism; and the relatively autonomous and deliberate *practices* and *devices* of abstraction (scientific, mathematical, linguistic, but also political and *juridical*) that are either articulated with real abstraction or posed by it as its 'presuppositions'. The problem of the creation and use of racial difference within practices of accumulation and dispossession, and its link to financialized abstraction and property law, in the case under consideration, would thus require not a reduction or integration, but an articulation of different modalities of abstraction, including race itself as an abstraction. 'Racism', writes Ruth Wilson Gilmore, 'is a practice of abstraction, a death-dealing displacement of difference into hierarchies that organize relations within and between the planet's sovereign political territories.' Processes of abstraction, Gilmore notes, figure humans in relation to inhuman persons in a hierarchy that produces the totalizing category of the 'human being'.[27]

We take this notion of articulation from the work of Stuart Hall in the late 1970s and early 1980s, in particular from his theoretical and political interventions into contemporary debates about Marxist method, interventions which centred on the question of race. Besides testaments to Hall's capacious scope and the generous engagement with a welter of different positions, these texts are unique in taking the different formations of race within capitalism as the impetus to rethink Marx's method of abstraction, and vice versa. In this regard, they can be said not only to address the varieties of racialized capitalism, in a way which can hopefully elucidate the place of property within them; they also offer vital perspectives through which to revisit those problems of abstraction and concreteness most memorably outlined in Marx's '1857 Introduction', a text to which Hall returned time and again.[28]

Though it is not possible to do much justice to Hall's insights here, we can note that his return to Marx's dialectic of the abstract and the concrete via Althusser's theory of overdetermination was aimed at generating a

Marxist theory capable of truly thinking difference. Against an ultra-Hegelian reading of Marx that would view his mature work through the lens of the self-movement of capital's categories, Hall stressed that Marx's were concepts 'which *differentiate* in the very moment that they reveal hidden connections'; though capitalism 'tends to reproduce itself in expanded form *as if* it were a self-equilibrating and self-sustaining system',[29] it constantly relies on precarious social and political mediations, including racisms themselves, none of which are guaranteed by an ineluctable logic. Though Hall, unlike many of his peers, does not jettison the notion of totality, he repeatedly asserts that capitalist social formations are complexly structured differentiated totalities, unities that require differentiation, in which, to use Neil Smith's formulation, the production of sameness or equivalence is always accompanied by a production of difference. From the Althusser of *For Marx* (which Hall plays off against what he perceived as the overly rigid structuralism of *Reading Capital*), he draws 'the recognition that there are different social contradictions with different origins; that the contradictions which drive the historical process forward do not always appear in the same place, and will not always have the same historical effects'.[30] Hall's counterintuitive avowal that Althusser 'enabled me to live in and with *difference*'[31] is brought home by his autobiographical analysis of the contrasting overdeterminations of class by race in the UK and Jamaica, and of the ways in which these different structurations-in-dominance – one in which the immigrant 'black' was starkly opposed to the native 'white', the other in which 'black' sat at one end of a spectrum in which 'white' was the absent apex – shaped everyday life and discourse.[32] Hall's insistence that in certain societies race can be the way 'the modality in which class is "lived", the medium through which class relations are experienced, the form in which it is appropriated and "fought through"',[33] is here compounded by the account, bolstered by a Marxism of difference, of how the abstract categories or systems of representations attached to race are experienced. The abstractions of race are in this regard not just real, but lived. This is among the reasons why 'there is nothing simple about the dynamics of racism.'[34]

Applied to the problem of race in capitalism, Althusser's concepts of articulation, overdetermination, and of societies structured-in-dominance, permitted Hall, by his own account, to undermine the teleological reductivism and economism of a certain Marxism – which would see race inevitably dissolved by class contradiction – as well as culturalist or ethnocentric accounts which treated race and racism as purely autonomous variables.[35] Both of these positions elide the historical specificity, which is also to say the political cognizability, of social formations in which race plays a structuring role. They helped Hall to think, especially in the collaborative project *Policing the Crisis*, how

> the structures through which black labour is reproduced ... are not simply 'coloured' by race: they work through race. The relations of capitalism can be thought of as articulating classes in distinct

> ways at each of the levels of instances of the social formation – economic, political, ideological. These levels are the "effects" of the structures of modern capitalist production, with the necessary displacement of relative autonomy operating between them.[36]

We would like to propose that contemporary debates on race and property could also be thought according to this model, to detail the ways in which property law also *works through race*,[37] and to investigate how, to use Hall's terms, the absence of any necessary correspondence between race and class, or race and property, by no means entails 'necessarily no correspondence' between them.[38]

At stake in thinking about legal forms as both *articulated with* and an *articulation of* economic and social relations, is continuing the excavation of how capitalist property relations preserve and rely upon 'other relations that are not ascribable within the "social relations of production." These include distinctions at the level of culture and values' – maintained by institutional structures, particular forms of political power, and of course, histories of colonization and slavery. For example, in commenting on the work of sociologists such as John Rex writing in the 1970s about South Africa, Hall notes that specifically colonial modes of labour were foundational to the establishment of a capitalist market economy:

> The 'origin' of the capitalist mode in conditions of conquest, coupled with the 'peculiar institutions' of unfree labour thus preserve, at the economic level, and secure its continuing racially ascriptive features. This is a capitalism of a very specific and distinctive kind: 'there are a number of different relationships to the means of production *more subtle than can be comprehended in terms of distinction between owners and non-owners*' each of which 'gives rise to specific class situations... a whole range of class situations.'[39]

Both before and after Hall's writing, the articulation of different strategies of accumulation, embedded in colonial modes of land appropriation, feudal social relations, and free and unfree labour, conceived of as constituting the mode through which legal forms of property and relations of ownership take root, has been undertaken by many scholars writing in the black radical tradition and indigenous studies. It is to them that we now turn.

Race, dispossession and the subject of property

At the turn of the twentieth century, Peruvian socialist Jose Mariátegui wrote incisively of the dispossession of Indian communities in Peru as the ground upon which the *latifundistas* built an agrarian economy that largely failed, in his view, to escape feudal social relations. Nonetheless, this was a feudalism that contained within it an 'incipient capitalism.'[40] Mariátegui posited the 'Indian land question' as one that was inherently economic, while also identifying those social and cultural aspects of 'indigenous communism' that were so severely diminished by the gradual imposition of colonial capitalist land ownership. Roxanne Dunbar-Ortiz has also identified the dispossession of indigenous lands as the central motor force of primitive accumulation in the United States.[41]

Dunbar-Ortiz maps the conquest of New Mexico through an exploration of three different but interlocking modes of ongoing capitalist expropriation: primitive accumulation based on the appropriation of native land, the appropriation of key resources, namely water, and the exploitation of native labour on the large estates, which was facilitated by successive imposition of non-native property law and land tenure and military occupation. Dunbar-Ortiz reveals how, contrary to orthodox Marxist understandings of the development of capitalism, the 'expropriation of the land, the means of production, and the resources' of the indigenous population, including their labour, are each coterminous with the development of agrarian capitalism in the USA, and continue into the present. We could also mention here the work of Silvia Federici,[42] Glen Coulthard,[43] and Ruth Wilson Gilmore, as demonstrating how contemporary capitalist accumulation relies on an amalgam of older and newer inventive mechanisms that preserve racial and gendered logics established during colonial settlement and slavery. In her landmark book, *The Golden Gulag*, Ruth Wilson Gilmore explores the many different economies involved in the intensification of incarceration in California. She examines how chronic unemployment and deindustrialization, planning laws, the use of financial instruments by public authorities to generate revenue, and of course a racial moral panic about crime, provided the fertile ground for prison expansion in California. Crucially, Wilson Gilmore illuminates the human cost of the forms of expropriation detailed in the book, emphasizing that entire ways of life are unmoored by capital flight.[44]

Employing the framework of articulation as a way of understanding contemporary forms of dispossession also offers one way of addressing the very salient question of legal subjectivity. As noted above, Hall endorses John Rex's observation that the distinction between owner and non-owner is no longer adequate, if it ever was, fully to understand racialized capitalist social formations, and, we could say by extension, contemporary forms of property and relations of ownership. This is not only because legal forms of property have proliferated so intensely in late modernity, rendering the function of ownership somewhat ambiguous in relation to key functions traditionally ascribed by Marxist theorists to ownership, namely exclusive control over the means of production. Hall seconds this observation because when we examine the specificities of how historically embedded forms of racism and patriarchy overlapped with particular economic structures, the attributes normally ascribed to the 'owner' are much more complex. For instance, the individual self-interest of black property owners and their involvement in race-based land expropriation in the 1960s and 1970s can only be explained, as N.D.B. Connolly does in his book *A*

World More Concrete: Real Estate and the Remaking of Jim Crow South Florida, because of the long history of slavery and legalized racism that made property ownership the most prized path to full citizenship. In other words, merely seeing black property owners as driven by the same profit motive as white landlords, or employing an economically reductive analytical framework, truly fails to grasp what the meaning of ownership is for black landlords, given the social relations and histories of race and racism that have shaped the US real-estate market.

Connolly argues that immigrants, black land- and property-owners, and even indigenous people 'made tremendous investments in racial apartheid, largely in an effort to govern growing cities and to unleash the value of land as real estate'.[45] Exploitative landlord and tenant relations between black landlords and black tenants were triangulated through that 'white apex' we have already encountered in Hall, embodied concretely in the real property that signified full citizenship and political power. The ideology of ownership embraced by these particular groups of people and individual landowners was mediated through histories of dispossession and displacement. The concept of the self-possessive individual that is variously assumed and critiqued by Marxist scholars also requires a deconstruction that takes into account the persistence of racism configured through relations of ownership. Scholars such as Saidiya Hartman have foregrounded C.B. Macpherson's failure to account for the history of slavery and, subsequent to that, Jim Crow laws that formed the conditions in which the ideal-typical possessive individual came into being. Hartman has argued that freedom from slavery, which granted former slaves entry into the framework of possessive individualism as free subjects, entailed a cruel contradiction. Self-possession was characterized, for instance, by the taking of a surname, often that of the ex-master, that 'conferred ... the paradox of emancipation and the dispossession that acquires the status of a legacy'.[46] Moving from the status of an object to that of a labouring subject was marked by debt peonage and labour conditions so brutal that they could hardly be said to reflect the alienation of one's labour through free choice.[47] As Hartman writes, '[t]he propertied person remained vulnerable to the dispossession exacted by violation, domination, and exploitation' that existed during slavery.[48] This is the recent history that informs present ideologies of ownership and the cultural and social significance of ownership for people of color in the USA, and particularly within black and indigenous communities.

The notion of 'articulation' also opens up the figure of the self-possessive individual to considering the colonially inscribed concepts of race in the fashioning of the modern legal subject. Balibar's *Identity and Difference* has begun to bridge the long-standing gap between Locke's theory of consciousness in the *Essay on Human Understanding* and his theory of property elaborated in the *Two Treatises of Government*.

How might Balibar's reflections on Locke assist us in accounting for the place of race and patriarchy in the identity-property nexus, or the contact point between propriety and property? In drawing out and emphasizing the temporal dimension of Locke's concept of self-consciousness, the concept of the self in the *Essay* not only moves closer to the political philosophy of property in the *Two Treatises of Government*, but bears traits or qualities that mirror Lockean concepts of property and ownership. Balibar argues here that the connection between identity and property ownership is relational, encompassing both an interiority of the self and the exteriority of the world (and social relations) outside of it. This relational aspect of the self in Locke's thought mirrors the relational nature of property itself, an ideational concept that travels between an ontological plane and the exterior world of relations of ownership.

In this expansive reading of Locke, Balibar outlines a theory of *constituent* property; an 'originary property' that is not 'measured' by pre-existing institutions because it is 'individuality itself'. With constituent property, 'property as such is the exercise of liberty' in the sense that 'every free man must always be considered *somehow a proprietor, or an "owner" of something*' which is individuality itself. Individuality, as noted above, is constituted through the self-recognition of one's memory of past and present thoughts. The idea that every man has property in himself brings propriety back into contact with property; or, to put it another way, Balibar presents a theory of a relation between constituted property and constituent property. The proper subject is not only he who actually owns property, or is able to 'freely' alienate his labour, but is, fundamentally, he who has the capacity to engage in the conscious reflection that marks out or defines the internal stage, 'an indefinitely open field in which [self-consciousness] is both actor and spectator'.[49]

Here we can attempt to identify the ways in which a racial anthropology of the human is smuggled into the ontological grounding of the possessive individual. The primary place of interiority in the conceptualization of this subject – one version of Spivak's 'transparent "I"' – sets the scene for an analytic of raciality that emerges in the nineteenth century. By locating the sovereign source of the self in Reason, Ferreira da Silva finds 'the negation, the declaration of the onto-epistemological inexistence of, exterior things, that is, the affirmation that, as objects of knowledge, phenomena, they constitute but effects of the interior tools of "pure reason".'[50] Racial subjects – the black slave, the Native, the savage – are located in an exterior realm of Nature by scientific and philosophical discourses that give primacy to the subject of interiority. Ferreira da Silva intervenes in our understanding of how the relationship between interiority and exteriority – as a defining characteristic of the modern subject – is mapped onto the globe and world history, so as to render most inhabitants of the non-European world as mere effects of the powers of Reason, which lie in the sole custody of their European superiors.

Taking the self-possessive individual back to the somewhat more specific scene of American real estate, it becomes evident that this articulation of specific histories of race and modes of possession – or, to be more specific, the social relations of race and class that are reflected in practices of redlining and the changes in lending practices – can quite easily become disarticulated from the crisis caused by the financialization of mortgage-backed securities, making the confluence of race and financialization seem more coincidental than a structurally integrated form of articulation, one critical to the reproduction of the US capitalist social order. For instance, in Gary Dymski's article 'Racial Exclusion and the Political Economy of the Subprime Crisis', the author analyses how redlining practices led to the 'creation of a multi-racial community-based movement' that advocated for an increase in mortgage financing for low-income 'minority' households.[51] This would allow for wealth accumulation through home ownership. Dymski poses the question, from a 'capital-accumulation perspective ... why would profit-seeking firms not set aside racial bias and make profitable loans' to minority households? He then states the following:

> Two responses suggest plausible explanations of this paradox. First, while lenders seek profits, most lending institutions and lending officers are non-minority, and thus susceptible to perceptual racial bias (despite their commitment to profit-maximization). Second, the perceived risks associated with lending in minority areas and to minorities are sufficiently great to deter lending.[52]

We want to suggest that these 'plausible explanations' actually disarticulate the racial foundations of property ownership in the US real-estate market. Long histories of racial-economic dispossession are sidelined, and instead racial prejudice as a generalized, almost transhistorical, phenomenon is offered as an explanation for race-based lending practices alongside the 'rational discrimination' argument. Similarly, the explanation for why racial exclusion was then replaced in part by extortionary racial inclusion in the form of subprime loans is reduced down to a matter of economics. And while greed certainly does explain a lot, it does not adequately account for how these lending practices exploited the social and cultural significance of ownership for communities who had not only been denied the credit facility, but for whom full juridical subjectivity and political inclusion had been denied on the basis of a certain ideal figure of the possessive individual, and, practically and historically speaking, had been defined in opposition to the black slave as object of ownership. In other words, how predatory lending targeted communities in which race is lived through property (along with class and gender), and vice versa.

This brings us to the greatest challenge for thinking race and class formations in relation to ownership through Marxian categories of analysis. Ownership, for black people in the USA, for indigenous people throughout North America, and for working-class immigrants, has always been refracted through the value of life itself, not reducible down to the category or reality of labour, be it free or unfree. If freedom was and remains bound to a debt that can never, it seems, be fully paid off, it seems that justice might require a disarticulation of the fetishes produced by racial and propertied abstractions, a *de-propertization* of the thinking of racial difference and of the legal form itself.

This article is a revised version of a paper given at the 'Powers and Limits of Property' workshop, organised by the Centre for Philosophy and Critical Thought, Goldsmiths, University of London, 11 June 2015.

1 Karl Marx, *Grundrisse*, trans. Martin Nicolaus, Penguin, Harmondsworth, 1973, p. 164.

2 Paula Chakravartty and Denise Ferreira da Silva, 'Accumulation, Dispossession, and Debt: The Racial Logic of Global Capitalism – An Introduction', *American Quarterly*, vol. 64, no. 3, September 2012, p. 362.

3 See, for example, Elvin K. Wyly, Mona Atia, Holly Foxcroft, Daniel J. Hamme and Kelly Phillips-Watts, 'American Home: Predatory Mortgage Capital and Neighbourhood Spaces of Race and Class Exploitation in the United States', *Geografiska Annaler: Series B, Human Geography*, vol. 88, no. 1, March 2006, pp. 105–32.

4 Elvin K. Wyly and Steven R. Holloway, 'Invisible Cities: Geography and the Disappearance of "Race" from Mortgage-Lending Data in the USA', *Social and Cultural Geography*, vol. 3, no. 3, 2002, pp. 247–82.

5 Marx, *Grundrisse*, p. 497.

6 Ibid, p. 498.

7 Ibid., p. 502.

8 Karl Marx, 'Economic and Philosophical Manuscripts', in *Marx and Engels Collected Works*, Lawrence & Wishart, London, 1986, p. 267.

9 Alfred Sohn-Rethel, *Intellectual and Manual Labour: A Critique of Epistemology*, Macmillan, London, 1978, p. 33.

10 See, among others, Peter Linebaugh, *Stop, Thief!: The Commons, Enclosure, and Resistance*, PM Press, Oakland CA, 2014; Michael Hardt and Antonio Negri, *Commonwealth*, Harvard University Press, Cambridge MA, 2011; Pierre Dardot and Christian Laval, *Commun. Essai sur la révolution au XXIe siècle, La Découverte*, Paris, 2015; Ugo Mattei, *Il benecomunismo e i suoi nemici*, Einaudi, Turin, 2015; Stefano Rodotà, *Il terribile diritto. Studi sulla proprietà privata e i beni comuni, il Mulino*, Milan, 2013.

11 Olivier Cayla and Yan Thomas, *Du droit de ne pas naître. À propos de l'affaire Perruche*, Gallimard, Paris, 2002, quoted by Giorgio Agamben in 'Tra il diritto e la vita', preface to Yan Thomas, I*l valore delle cose*, ed. Michele Spanò, Quodlibet, Macerata, 2015, p. 11. This Italian volume is built around the translation of Yan Thomas, 'La valeur des choses. Le droit romain hors la religion', *Annales HSS*, November–December 2002, pp. 1431–62.

12 Thomas, cited by Agamben, 'Tra il diritto e la vita', p. 13.

13 Thomas, *Il valore delle cose*, p. 24.

14 The latter are to be distinguished in turn from *res nullius*, 'awaiting' appropriation.

15 Thomas, *Il valore delle cose*, pp. 66, 79.

16 Michele Spanò, afterword to Thomas, *Il valore delle cose*, p. 89.

17 Thomas, *Il valore delle cose*, p. 56.

18 Karl Marx, 'On Proudhon' [Letter to J.B. Schweitzer], in *Marx and Engels Collected Works*, vol. 20, Lawrence & Wishart, London, 1985, pp. 27–8.

19 Karl Marx, 'Moralising Criticism and Critical Morality', in *Marx and Engels Collected Works*, vol. 6, Lawrence & Wishart, London, 1976, p. 337.

20 This lag between 'real' property, or property as a power, and legal property, was thought crucial to think the problems of transition, whether from feudalism to capitalism, or capitalism to socialism.

21 Nicos Poulantzas, 'The Problem of the Capitalist State', in *The Poulantzas Reader*, ed. James Martin, Verso, London, 2008, p. 177.

22 Étienne Balibar, 'The Basic Concepts of Historical Materialism', in Louis Althusser and Étienne Balibar, *Reading Capital* (1968), trans. Ben Brewster, Verso, London, 1979, p. 230.

23 Here the Balibar of *Reading Capital* also seems to be leaning towards a view of law as real abstraction not miles away from Pashukanis's *General Theory of Law and Marxism*.

24 Étienne Balibar, 'Plus-value et classes sociales: Contribution à la critique de l'économie politique', in *Cinq études de materialisme historique*, François Maspéro, Paris, 1974, p. 163 n65.

25 Paul Hirst, 'The Law of Property and Marxism', in *On Law and Ideology*, Macmillan, London, 1979, p. 98.

26 Ibid., p. 137.

27 Ruth Wilson Gilmore, 'Fatal Couplings of Power and Difference: Notes on Racism and Geography', *The Professional Geographer*, vol. 54, no. 1, 2002, pp. 15–24; p. 16.

28 See especially Stuart Hall, 'Marx's Notes on Method: A "Reading" of the "1857 Introduction"', *Cultural Studies*, vol. 17, no. 2, 2003, pp. 113–49. This text was originally published in 1974 in *Working Papers in Cultural Studies*, the journal of the Centre for Contemporary Cultural Studies in Birmingham.

29 Ibid., pp. 118, 125.

30 Stuart Hall, 'Signification, Representation, Ideology: Althusser and the Post-Structuralist Debates', *Critical Studies in Mass Communication*, vol. 2, no. 2, June 1985, p. 92.

31 Ibid.

32 In 'Signification, Representation, Ideology', Hall employs this Althusserian framework to shed light on two painful family stories, two 'interpellations' of sorts, the first having to do with his Jamaican mother's exclamation 'I hope they don't mistake you over there [in Britain] for one of those immigrants', the second with the family tale that his sister had looked into his crib and asked 'Where did you get this Coolie baby from?' Hall writes: 'From that moment onwards, my place within this system of reference has been problematic. It may help to explain why and how I eventually became what I was first nominated: the "Coolie" of the family, the one who did not fit, the outsider, the one who hung around the street with all the wrong people, and grew up with all those funny ideas. The Other one.' (p. 110). John Akomfrah's film *The Stuart Hall Project* (2013) also touches on these experiences.

33 Stuart Hall, 'Race, Articulation and Societies Structured in Dominance', in *Sociological Theories: Race and Colonialism*, UNESCO, Paris, 1980, p. 341. Earlier, Hall had observed that 'racial oppression was the specific mediation through which this class experienced its material and cultural conditions of life, and hence race formed the central mode through which the self-consciousness of the class stratum could be constructed.' Stuart Hall, Chas Critcher, Tony Jefferson, John Clarke and Brian Roberts, *Policing the Crisis: Mugging, The State and Law and Order*, Macmillan, London, 1978, p. 387.

34 Stuart Hall, 'Race, Culture, and Communications: Looking Backward and Forward at Cultural Studies', *Rethinking Marxism*, vol. 5, no. 1, 1992, p. 15.

35 '[O]ne cannot explain racism in abstraction from other social relations – even if, alternatively, one cannot explain it by reducing it to those relations.' Hall, 'Race, Articulation and Societies Structured in Dominance', p. 337.

36 Ibid., p. 340.

37 Though Hall does not elaborate upon the property-race relationship, he does comment on 'juridical racism' and on the 'ideological work' required for plantation slavery to persist as a kind of enclave in societies predicated on other legal and property forms. Hall, 'Race, Articulation and Societies Structured in Dominance', p. 338.

38 Hall defines articulation as 'a connection or link which is not necessarily given in all cases, as a law or fact of life, but which requires particular conditions of existence to appear at all, which has to be positively sustained by specific processes, which is not "eternal" but has constantly to be renewed, which can under some circumstances disappear or be overthrown, leading to the old linkages being dissolved and new connections – re-articulations – being forged. It is also important that an articulation between different practices does not mean that they become identical or that the one is dissolved into the other. Each retains its distinct determinations and conditions of existence; the two practices can function together, not as an "immediate identity" (in the language of Marx's "1857 Introduction") but as "distinctions within a unity"' (pp. 113–14). See also 'Race, Articulation and Societies Structured in Dominance', pp. 326–30.

39 Hall, 'Race, Articulation and Societies Structured in Dominance', p. 311; our emphasis.

40 José Carlos Mariátegui, 'The Land Problem' (1928), in *An Anthology*, ed. Harry E. Vanden and Marc Becker, Monthly Review Press, New York, 2011, p. 72.

41 Roxanne Dunbar-Ortiz, *An Indigenous Peoples' History of the United States*, Beacon Press, Boston MA, 2015; see also her *Roots of Resistance: A History of Land Tenure in Mexico*, University of Oklahoma Press, Norman, 2007.

42 Silvia Federici, *Caliban and the Witch: Women, the Body and Primitive Accumulation*, Autonomedia, New York, 2004; see also 'Women, Land Struggles, and Globalization: An International Perspective', in *Revolution at Point Zero: Housework, Reproduction, and Feminist Struggle*, PM Press, Oakland CA, 2012.

43 Glen Coulthard, Red Skin, *White Masks: Rejecting the Colonial Politics of Recognition*, University of Minnesota Press, Minneapolis, 2014.

44 Ruth Wilson Gilmore, *Golden Gulag: Prisons, Surplus, Crisis, and Opposition in Globalizing California*, University of California Press, Berkeley CA, 2007, p. 179.

45 N.D.B. Connolly, *A World More Concrete: Real Estate and the Remaking of Jim Crow South Florida*, University of Chicago Press, Chicago, 2014, p. 3.

46 Saidiya Hartman, *Scenes of Subjection: Terror, Slavery, and Self-Making in Nineteenth-Century America*, Oxford University Press, Oxford, 1997, p. 155.

47 Ibid., p. 135.

48 Ibid., p. 134.

49 Étienne Balibar, *Identity and Difference: John Locke and the Invention of Consciousness*, Verso, London, 2013, pp. 14–15.

50 Denise Ferreira da Silva, *Toward a Global Idea of Race*, University of Minnesota Press, Minneapolis, 2007, pp. 60–61.

51 Gary Dymski, 'Racial Exclusion and the Political Economy of the Subprime Crisis', *Historical Materialism*, vol. 17, no. 2, 2009, p. 153.

52 Ibid., p. 154.

Acknowledgements

Bruno Zhu is deeply grateful to all the authors for their visionary insights and grace which inspired the genesis of this reader series, and to Alisa Heil, Alivia Zivich, Anna Susanna Woof, Enver Hadzijaj, Giulia Damiani, Joni Zhu, Kah Bee Chow, Lisette Smits, Melanie Bühler, Olivia Aherne, Rachel Be-Yun Wang, and Chisenhale Gallery for their unflinching support while conceiving this volume. Zhu extends his gratitude to Amy Jones, Anna-Sophie Berger, Cory John Scozzari, Daniel Sperry, Jasmine Gregory, Jeppe Ugelvig, Mahan Moalemi, Marina Xenofontos, and Pieter Verbeke for saying, doing, sharing things, thoughts, and words that sparked unexpected breakthroughs.

Bruno Zhu lives and works between Portugal and The Netherlands. His work has been presented in exhibitions across Rotterdam, Hong Kong and Detroit, amongst others, and published by San Serriffe and 5b. He is a member of A Maior, a curatorial program set in a home furnishings and clothing store in Viseu, Portugal.

Credits

Staff

Oscar Abdulla
Assistant Curator
Tom Adriani
Technician
Olivia Aherne
Curator
Henrietta Armstrong
Technician
Millie Barretta
Front of House and Events Coordinator
Alex Blackbourn
Operations Manager
Dani Chamorro
Front of House and Events Assistant
Charlotte Cole
Deputy Director
Georgina Corrie
Finance Manager
Grant Foster
Technician
Alessia Franchi
Technician
Anaïs Goorriah
Events Assistant
Yifan He
Front of House and Events Assistant
Hampus Hoh
Events Assistant
Charlie Howard
Front of House and Events Assistant
Rosie Kennedy
Technician
Zeynep Koksal
Communications Assistant
Zethu Maseko
Events Assistant
Giorgio Mattia
Senior Development Manager
Paulina Michnowska
Technician
Edwin Mingard
Chisenhale TECHNE Collaborative Doctoral Fellow
Duncan Morris
Technician
Jen O'Farrell
Events Assistant
Tolu Oshodi
Events Assistant
Grace Page
Front of House and Events Assistant
Seth Pimlott
Curator: Social Practice
Clare Rees-Hales
Technician
Caoimhe Rogan
Development Coordinator
Adam Shield
Technician
Heena Song
Events Assistant
Josie Spalla
Digital and Communications Manager
Nkara Stephenson
Events Assistant
Rachel Be-Yun Wang
Asymmetry Curatorial Research Fellow
Zoé Whitley
Director
Daniel Wilkinson
Technician
Lucy Woodhouse
Head Technician

Exhibtion Credits

License to Live is produced and commissioned by Chisenhale Gallery, London.

Major Supporter
Cherry Xu

Lead Supporter
Embassy of the Kingdom of the Netherlands

With additional support from the Chisenhale Gallery Commissions Fund.

Chisenhale Gallery's Schools' Programme 2024 is made possible through the generosity of Goodman Gallery and Freelands Foundation.

The 2023–24 Asymmetry Curatorial Research Fellow is hosted by Chisenhale Gallery.

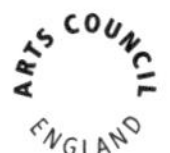

Supported using public funding by
ARTS COUNCIL ENGLAND

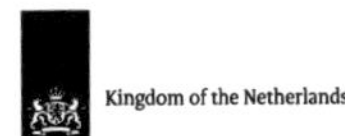

Colophon

Volume I of **Fiction Non Fiction** is published on the occasion of the exhibition **License to Live** by Bruno Zhu at Chisenhale Gallery, London (22 November 2024 – 2 February 2025).

Editors
Chisenhale Gallery
Bruno Zhu

Managing Editor
Anita Dawood

Publishing Editor
Micola Clara Brambilla

Design
Enver Hadzijaj

Texts

Foreword by Zoé Whitley

Introduction by Bruno Zhu

Gilroy, Paul. Excerpt from 'Lecture I: Suffering and Infrahumanity.' In *The Tanner Lectures on Human Values*, 34: 29–38. Salt Lake City: University of Utah Press, 2016.

Wynter, Sylvia. 'Novel and History, Plot and Plantation.' In *We Must Learn to Sit Down Together and Talk about a Little Culture: Decolonising Essays, 1967–1984*. Peepal Tree Press, 2022.
Reprinted with permission from Peepal Tree Press.

Britton, Celia. "Opacity and Transparence: Conceptions of History and Cultural Difference in the Work of Michel Butor and Edouard Glissant." *French Studies* 49, no. 3 (July 1, 1995): 308–20. https://doi.org/10.1093/fs/49.3.308.
Unless otherwise noted excerpts translated by Louise Darblay.
Reprinted with permission from Oxford University Press.

Madureira, Luís. "A Supplement to the White Man's Burden: Lobo Antunes, History, the Colonial Wars, and the April Revolution." *Portuguese Literary and Cultural Studies* 19/20 (2011): 227–46. https://doi.org/10.62791/p68ram11.

Excerpts translated by Bruno Zhu.

Lowe, Lisa. "Autobiography Out of Empire." In *The Intimacies of Four Continents*, 43–71. Duram, NC: Duke University Press, 2015. https://doi.org/10.1215/9780822375647.

Davis, Muriam Haleh. "Settler Entanglements from Citrus Production to Historical Memory." *Middle East Report* 302, 51, no. 1 (Spring 2022). https://merip.org/2022/05/settler-entanglements-from-citrus-production-to-historical-memory-2/.
Reprinted with permission from MERIP.

Federici, Silvia. "Woman, Land-Struggles and the Valorization of Labor." *The Commoner*, no. 10 (Spring/Summer 2005). https://thecommoner.org/wp-content/uploads/2020/06/Silvia-Federici-Women%E2%80%99s-Land-Struggles.pdf
Reprinted with permission from The Commoner.
thecommoner.org.uk

Bhandar, Brenna, and Alberto Toscano. "Race, Real Estate and Real Abstraction." *Radical Philosophy*, no. 194 (November 1, 2015). https://www.radicalphilosophyarchive.com/issue-files/rp194_dossier_propertypowerlaw_bandar_toscano.pdf.

First edition 2024

Co-published by Chisenhale Gallery, London and Mousse Publishing, Milan.

With the generous support of Frank Bowling and Rachel Scott.

64 Chisenhale Rd, Bow, London E3 5QZ
chisenhale.org.uk

Distributed by
Mousse Publishing
Contrappunto s.r.l.
via Pier Candido Decembrio 28
20137, Milan–Italy

Available through
Mousse Publishing, Milan
moussemagazine.it

Printed by Pureprint Group, UK

ISBN 9788867493111

£ 15 GBP / € 18 EUR / $ 20 USD

A catalogue record for this book is available from The British Library.